Slow Selling

By Guy Arnold and Brendan Donnelly

How to Get Customers Wanting to Buy Without Sacrificing Principles or Profits

....

Published by New Generation Publishing in 2019

Copyright © Guy Arnold and Brendan Donnelly 2019

First Edition

The author asserts the moral right under the Copyright, Designs and Patents Act 1988 to be identified as the author of this work.

All Rights reserved. No part of this publication may be reproduced, stored in a retrieval system or transmitted, in any form or by any means without the prior consent of the author, nor be otherwise circulated in any form of binding or cover other than that which it is published and without a similar condition being imposed on the subsequent purchaser.

You can become licensed to train and coach this material to others. For details see www.slow-selling.org

ISBNs:
        Paperback 978-1-78955-564-6
        Hardback 978-1-78955-565-3

www.newgeneration-publishing.com

New Generation Publishing

'Slow and steady wins the race': Aesop

'They stumble that run fast': Shakespeare.

'To build may have to be the thoughtful and laborious task of years. To destroy can be the thoughtless act of a single day': Churchill

'In relationships, slow is fast and fast is slow': Dr Stephen Covey

'It's important to slow down': Simon Sinek

…………………………..

Thankyou

Slow Selling has been a project that many have helped with: here are a few who we'd particularly like to thank: Alison Arnold, David Covey, Julian Richer, Seth Godin, Carl Honore, Geir Berthelsen, Paul Matthews, Jay Wright, David Young, Rupert Burnell-Nugent, Sara Daw, John Harvey, Peter Massey, Michael Heppell, Morris Pentel, Hyrum Smith, Scott Goodfellow, Grant Leboff, Derek Jones, George Edward-Collins and Ian Golding.

The 'Slow Selling' Authors

Guy

Guy started his career as a beer sales rep in Kent, UK.

After a varied career in the hospitality industry, both running his own award-winning businesses, and in senior levels in large organisations, he used his experience in turning around failing businesses to write his first book: 'Great or Poor'.

Guy now runs his own business support and advice business, specialising in effective sales, loyalty and reputation systems that help organisations continually build profits whilst also reducing unnecessary costs and problems.

Guy lives on Dartmoor, in Devon, UK with his wife Alison.

'Slow Selling' is Guy's 4th book.

Guy is also the founder of the 'Slow Sellers Association' www.slow-sellers.org

Brendan

Brendan left school in his native Cumbria at 16 with a clutch of O levels and a desire to work, after factory work and swimming coach, he gained a degree from Lancaster University and has held a variety of management positions, predominantly dealing with sales. With his wife Cherry, he has also set up 3 businesses (2 successful 1 not so much), whilst learning all the time.

Very much hands on, Brendan has sold a wide variety of product from crisps to concepts, earth moving equipment to cake, and glazing to cleaning products. He is based in the North Midlands and tries hard now to achieve the correct work life balance.

Brendan's friendship with Guy dates back over 30 years and is strengthened by the shared belief that the current sales models are broken and ineffective, resulting in this collaboration that attempts to address the imbalance and properly put the customer at the centre of the sales model.

For more information please contact us via www.slow-selling.org

'Slow Selling' is a simple set of principles, tools and processes that enables you to slow down, stop panicking and focus on what's truly effective for the long term in your world.

So you can feel confident to do the things you know in your heart are 'right' with the conviction that this will also bring you financial success, no matter how tough your market is, or how hungry your competition.

By doing these things, you will develop a line of eager customers wanting to buy from you, enjoy fiercely loyal customers who want to buy more and more, and benefit from huge levels of customer reputation and attraction.

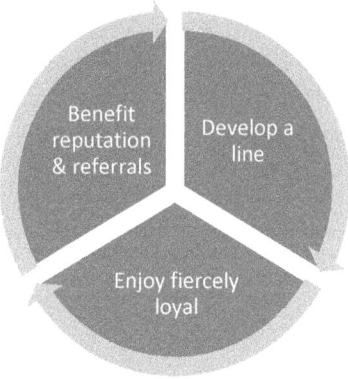

'You have to do the right things first, then the customers will want to give you their money ... not the other way round!' *Guy Arnold, Founder of the Slow Selling Movement.*

Please Note:

For the sake of clarity and simplicity, this book is written from the point of view of your relationship, as an individual, team or organisation, with the external customer.

*But, please remember: as a Manager or Leader, **your primary customers are your people**: treat them better than you treat your best customer and they'll do the same for the external customer. If you are reading this as a Manager or Leader, use the ideas, principles and tools to engage and develop your relationship with your people first, then work with them as a team, using the same ideas, principles and tools, to engage and develop your relationship with your external customers.*

Slow Selling
List of contents

Opinions on 'Slow Selling'.. i

Introduction xv

Preface.. 1

Part 1: Introduction and Background 7

    The key start point: 9

    What is 'Selling'? 9

    We are social animals.. 13

    The major change in communication................................... 13

    Hunter / Gatherers 15

    Slow Down! 16

    Every customer is a long-term high value one in the customer empowered world 19

    Which means that 22

    The problem with 'traditional selling' 26

    'Slow Selling' is the '3rd Alternative'!..................................... 28

    There are 5 outcomes to a Sales Process (and not all of them are great!)... 29

    ABC changes to ABH 32

    'Sellers' and 'Servers' 34

Part 2: The Four Principles of Human Behaviour 37

    BELIEFS, EMOTIONS, ACTIONS, RESULTS…… (B.E.A.R.s)....... 39

    BELIEFS 41

    EMOTIONS 43

    ACTIONS 46

    RESULTS 49

    Slow Selling … no matter what situation you're in 52

Part 3: Selling Beliefs 55

    Making money 57

    Having a strong pitch 62

    Sales Processes and Techniques are Key 65

    Pushy..68

    Marketing drives sales 71

    Advertise 73

    First impressions 75

    The customer is always right...77

    The seller is in control (in B2C situations).............................80

    The buyer is in control (in B2B situations) 82

    Linear sales processes...84

    Hidden agendas 87

    The sales and marketing funnel 90

    CRM systems..93

    After sales follow up 95

    After sales e-selling 99

    Direct and Indirect Response Systems................................102

    Testimonials 105

    Doing Feedback in the right way...107

Part 4: Selling emotions..109

Uncover needs 111

Sell benefits 114

Product Features 119

Find Solutions 121

Overcoming objections 124

Tell / lead the customer 127

Don't tell them unless they ask 129

Special introductory offers 132

Complicated pricing 134

Limited guarantees 136

Part 5: Selling Actions 139

Opening techniques 140

E-Marketing 143

Demonstrate capability 145

Probe 148

Give demonstrations / send proposals 150

Close 153

Closing techniques 155

Get a commitment 159

Leading questions 162

Open and closed questions 165

Closing 167

Cold calling 169

Email selling / PPC / Targeted Ads 173

Electronic 'Smart' Selling 176

Sales & Discounts 178

Free! 181

Solutions 185

After sales techniques 188

Getting referrals and introductions 192

A 'great' referral system: 194

An easy inch-by-inch approach to approaching a Referee .196

Overcoming 'Objections' when you approach a referee 200

Part 6. Selling Measures 203

The Problem 204

Measures 204

Incentivise 207

A short rant on Measures! 209

For the record 211

Part 7: SLOW SELLING: a simple guide to getting it right 213

BELIEFS 215

Slow Start 215

Slow Targets 218

EMOTIONS 220

Slow Names 220

Slow Listening 220

ACTIONS & EMOTIONS 224

Slow Problem Solving 224

Slow Onion Peeling 225

Slow Value Creation 232

>   Slow Pricing 233
>
>   Slow Alternatives 235
>
>   Slow Facts and Measures... 236
>
>   Slow Outcomes 238
>
>   How to get to a slow outcome: the process 239
>
>   Slow Guarantees 240
>
>   EMOTIONS, RESULTS & ACTIONS 242
>
>   Slow Follow-Ups 242
>
>   Slow Feedback 242
>
>   Professional Feedback Systems: Key Rules 245
>
>   Slow loyalty 246
>
>   Slow repeat sales, up sales & cross sales 251
>
>   Slow Referrals 255

Part 8: Action Plan.. 257

Appendix 1: Win/win agreements 261

Appendix 2: Sample completed win/win agreement............. 263

Appendix 3: Action sheet for inch by inch improvement....... 269

Appendix 4: The 'Slow Sellers Oath'....................................... 273

Opinions on 'Slow Selling'

"Are you trying to sell me something?"

For a culture that spends so much time and money buying things, you'd think we'd be more excited when someone tries to sell us something.

But we're not.

The semantics are important here. What we really mean is, "are you trying to selfishly persuade me to buy something that will benefit you more than it benefits me?"

We're goal-directed, risk-averse and self-focused. We don't care about the salesperson's commission, of course. We care about our own resources.

The magic happens when the goals are aligned, when the service component of sales kicks in, when long-term satisfaction exceeds short-term urgency.

When someone acts in a way that says, "can I help you buy something?" or, "can I help you achieve your goals?" then we're on our way. And of course, it's the doing, not the saying that matters the most.

Seth Godin, *thought leader, blogger and best-selling Author*
www.sethgodin.com

The time has come to challenge our obsession with doing everything more quickly.

Speed is not always the best policy. Evolution works on the principle of survival of the fittest, not the fastest. Remember who won the race between the tortoise and the hare. As we hurry through life, cramming more into every hour, we are stretching ourselves to the breaking point

… this … is not a declaration of war against speed. Speed has helped to remake our world in ways that are wonderful and liberating. The problem is that our love of speed, our obsession with doing more and more in less and less time, has gone too far; it has turned into an addiction, a kind of idolatry. Even when speed starts to backfire, we invoke the go-faster gospel. Falling behind at work? Get a quicker Internet connection. Diet not working? Try liposuction. Too busy to cook? Buy a microwave. And yet some things cannot, should not, be sped up. They take time; they need slowness. When you accelerate things that should not be accelerated … there is a price to pay.

Carl Honoré*: Slow Movement Leader, and Author of multimillion selling 'In Praise of Slow'*
www.carlhonore.com

The quality of the product or service you sell is tantamount: you have to believe in it.

You also have to have the integrity and discipline at every level to make sure that you never compromise: everything about your product or service matters, there is no part of it that isn't important to your overall brand.

You need to work to make your brand premium, step by step, and you need to be brave enough to set out your stall and stick to it.

We will never compromise or reduce our quality: as soon as you compromise once you can never go back and then you can only rely on price and promotion in order to keep selling your products.

Slow Selling is a great concept: it's exactly what we've done over the years: we have always aimed to build a brand of quality, step by step, examining every step and making sure it's right, and never compromising. Everything matters: you need to develop everything slowly.

In the same way, you have to be rigorous with your people: you have to make sure everyone shares your vision and values and genuinely want to sign up to what we want to achieve. It's never quick fix: you have to build your team slowly and properly.

Paul Matthews, Sales Director, Timothy Taylor – Brewers of the World's most prize-winning beer, Landlord.
www.timothytaylor.co.uk

The Businesses that get it right

The businesses that get it right understand a few basic principles. They treat everyone well, not just because it's the right thing to do but because that's how you end up with friendly, knowledgeable staff serving customers who will want to come back. These are the principles promoted by 'Slow Selling'.

Julian Richer: Founder and Managing Director of Richer Sounds (Guinness World Record Holders for sales per square foot)
www.richersounds.com

You build business from the inside out.

'At Virgin Wines we believe you build businesses from the inside out, with the focus on employing outstanding people who care passionately about every aspect of the customer experience. Working relentlessly to deliver the very finest service has, in turn, led to a consistent and continual growth in sales. It is this exact approach that is advocated and explained in the 'Slow Selling' process. I thoroughly recommend this book!'

Jay Wright, CEO Virgin Wines
www.virginwines.co.uk

How can we be as valuable to our customers as possible?

At the FD Centre, our aim is for anyone we come into contact with to say behind our backs: 'Thank goodness I met them', whether we are actively working with customers or not. We do this by continually asking and stretching ourselves: how can we be as valuable to our customers as possible, and how can we do this in a way that makes their lives noticeably easier? These are exactly the principles put forward by 'Slow Selling'... And they really work!

Sara Daw, CEO, The FD Centre
www.thefdcentre.co.uk

Success isn't about a quick buck

'Success in the long run isn't about a quick buck, it's about getting customers to actively choose you over your competition, time and time again. Whether you're a little bit dearer or a little bit cheaper, the real value to them lies deeper than that. This is exactly what 'Slow Selling' is about, and it's kept us in business for almost 250 years'

David Young, Managing Director, Bradfords Building Supplies
www.bradfords.co.uk

The most important part of selling is...

I believe the most important part of selling is selling with the right intent. If the intent is correct, for example you genuinely believe in your product or service, you know you're the best, you are convinced the after-sale will deliver, then it's so easier to sell from the heart with real intent.

Buyers can tell if you are selling with true intent and trust you to make a sale and get your commission. After any sales process, it's worth asking, 'What was my intent?' If intuitively you were selling just to make the sale then maybe it's time to think about something else. If you're selling to genuinely improve the life of your customer then keep going!

The ideas in Slow Selling are all about how to sell with good intent: I really like the idea of 'Slow Selling'.

Michael Heppell: Top Motivational Speaker, Success Coach and bestselling Author
www.michaelheppell.com

Start with the intention of creating a great reputation.

When we started our business, we started with the intention of creating a genuinely great reputation, high levels of repeat custom, and a place where travellers would go out of their way to visit: this is exactly the process that's outlined in 'Slow Selling' ... and it works!

Rupert Burnell-Nugent, MD, Hog & Hedge
www.hogandhedge.co.uk

Sales has never been easy, but now it's harder than ever.

Effective selling has never been easy, but now, in the world of the empowered customer and transparent business reputation, it's harder than ever. This more stringent world calls for much simpler and more customer focused sales tools and processes, and 'Slow Selling' delivers exactly that.

Hyrum Smith, Co-Founder and former CEO of Franklin Covey, bestselling Business and Effectiveness Author
https://www.hyrumwsmith.com/

If we are going to do anything, we want to do it well.

At Wilkin & Sons our approach is pretty simple really. We make the best products that we can, we treat people with respect, and we look after our environment. We are always on the lookout for new opportunities, and if we are going to do anything, we want to do it well. We know this is sometimes seen as 'old fashioned' or 'slow', but it serves us well and it's an approach we're proud to promote.

Scott Goodfellow, Managing Director, Wilkin & Sons
www.tiptree.com

'Slow Selling' is a breath of fresh air.

"Slow Selling is a breath of fresh air. Today's traditional sales approaches are broken, outdated and obsolete. Guy and Brendan offer a breakthrough approach that if implemented will revolutionize how selling should be done in the 21st century. I highly recommend this book. In selling, we all need to remind ourselves that fast is slow and slow is fast. This book will show you how to do it.

David M. R. Covey, CEO of SMCOV & co-author of Trap Tales: Outsmarting the 7 Hidden Obstacles to Success
https://www.davidmrcovey.com/

Sellers need to act in a slower, more considered and more sophisticated way.

Many of the traditional methods of selling are way out of date: prospects have much more choice than ever before, and are going through more of the purchase journey on their own. Sellers need to act in a slower, more considered and sophisticated way: they need to add value to the buyer at every step. This is exactly the message and tools delivered by 'Slow Selling'.

Grant Leboff, Bestselling author of 'Sticky Marketing' and international marketing and sales expert
www.stickymarketing.com

Modern Sales People need to be highly skilled relationship builders.

The days of sales staff bombarding their prospects with jargon and fancy closes are thankfully a distant memory.

Today we live in a service world: our sales focus can never again be 'sell and forget', our emphases and related business successes are based upon customer lifetime value.

Modern sales people need to be highly skilled long-term relationship builders, they need to fully appreciate a true consultative approach to selling, this takes time and professional training.

Guy is an expert in the art of modern selling techniques, his books and information around 'sales through service' are simply second to none and I very much look forward to educating my sales team through his new book 'Slow Selling'

Derek Jones *Founder & Chairman, Synaxon UK Ltd*
www.synaxon.co.uk

Slowing down to get it right from the start is the smartest business strategy there is.

Slowing down to get it right from the start is the smartest business strategy there is because it is vitally important to ensure that the entire organisation is aligned….. to the business AND customer experience strategies. You might think these are one and the same, but too often, organisations are very clear in defining what the business wants, but less clear on connecting that to what the customer wants. Creating a balanced strategy that connects both business AND customer objectives will not just boost sales for the benefit of the business, it will enable the delivery of consistently better customer AND employee experiences

Ian Golding, Global Customer Experience Specialist and author of 'Customer What? The honest and practical guide to customer experience
www.ijgolding.com

Treat your customer in the same way as your best friend.

If you treat your customer in the same way as you'd treat your best friend, they'll want to spend their money with you, and not only that, they'll want to persuade their friends to do the same. This is exactly the approach put forward by 'Slow Selling'.

Mark Godfrey, MD, The Deer Park Hotel, multi award winning Hotelier
www.deerpark.co.uk

You need to take it slowly and learn by trial and error

SMEs have an advantage over large organisations, as they're closer to customers and can be more focused on this. They also now have access to a huge number of very powerful tools to manage customer relationships effectively for very low cost.

They need to stay away from complicated ideas: they need to take it slowly and learn by trial and error: relying on really good, simple, customer feedback all the time.

Slow Selling is a very practical approach that an Organisation can understand and apply easily.

Morris Pentel, Chairman of the CX foundation and MD escore.today
www.cxfo.org

Slow Selling is about being in the present moment.

'Slow Selling is about slowing down and being in the present moment for your customers. The root of the word 'branding' comes from Livestock branding, a technique for marking livestock in order to identify the owner. It is very easy to see if the owner really cared for his livestock or not. In the same way, your customer will see that your brand is the real thing because of the way you treat your customer here and now.

Geir Berthelsen, Founder, The World Institute of Slowness
www.theworldinstituteofslowness.com

The best sales model is about creating a desire to do business with you.

The best sales model is all about creating a desire to do business with you. The absolute key is making it easy for the customer. In order to do this well, there's a terrific amount of time, money and effort that needs to be invested behind the scenes. This is the approach set out in Slow Selling.

Peter Massey, CX and Loyalty Expert, MD Budd Uk Ltd
www.budd.uk.com

The traditional model of sales & marketing is fundamentally flawed.

The traditional model of sales & marketing is fundamentally flawed. The power now lies with the customer more than ever before as they are better informed and have endless choice. As a result, everything about your operation must be customer focused and their experience is key!

John Harvey, Founder, The Samphire Club
www.thesamphireclub.co.uk

Slow selling feels counterintuitive

Slow selling feels counterintuitive but by taking the time to understand a potential client and their needs it helps build trust and allows you to build a long-term relationship rather than a quick transaction with no future commitment. Sell slow and solve sales.

Andrew Ellis, Founder, Like Minds
www.wearelikeminds.com

Introduction

Not another book on selling!

Surely there are already too many books on 'selling', offering too many quick fix techniques?

Well, yes there are and that is exactly the problem… Too many quick fixes, too many top tips, too many 'this'll result in an avalanche of buyers' and over-hyped long-winded ideas, which deliver trickles of extra sales at best…

… And force you well out of your comfort zone …and into doing things you'd ordinarily be ashamed of at worst.

In other words, there is usually too much 'selling' – and not nearly enough 'creating true and long-lasting demand'.

Well this book is different… very different.

So what is the book about and why was it written?

In a nutshell, we were curious about:
- Why all the organisations we'd worked for, and worked with, were so obviously doing stupid things that annoyed customers and jeopardised their reputation, yet they failed to either see them or stop doing them.

- Why people at the front line in these organisations clearly see these problems and openly talk about them, yet the organisation fails to listen, take notice or act.

- Why so many organisations, large and small, start off well but then start to struggle as they get bigger.

- Why if customer attraction, loyalty, and reputation are simply a matter of common sense is common sense so rare in practice?

Simple changes

In all the businesses we've worked with, we've introduced some simple changes (slowly!) based on fundamental principles, which have made huge differences.

We have managed to generate significant and long-lasting improvements through some small changes and simple fixes for our clients.

So why isn't making small changes an obvious solution to every business leader and owner? What in reality is stopping this? And what are the simple principles and fixes we have seen and successfully implemented?

This book will answer those questions and give you the tools to make the necessary changes yourself.

Perspective

We suggest that it's all a matter of perspective: slowing down, identifying some fundamental key common sense principles and putting the systems, checks and balances in place, to ensure everyone sticks to them: through thick and thin, at all levels and without exception.

(That's the hard bit!)

As a customer of other businesses, we can all clearly see various issues, problems, and small glitches in their systems that stops them blowing our socks off and earning our enthusiastic loyalty. However, when we cease being a customer and start to work within a business, this perspective gets lost very quickly: instead, we start to focus on our internal pressures and issues in order to achieve our sales goals.

Slow Selling is a set of systems and tools to help individuals, teams, and businesses retain the perspective of the external customer. It also empowers them to continually develop and improve systems, inch by inch, using this perspective, so that over time they will consistently make your business stand out and be remarkable in the eyes of your customer.

This takes time: there are no short cuts or quick fixes: that's why it's called 'slow selling'.

Slowing down

In the rush to achieve turnover and profits, things that matter to customers often get missed, and even are deliberately ignored or ridiculed as being 'too soft' or 'not aligned with our targets'. Unfortunately finance managers and accountants are particularly guilty of doing this, because bottom-line profits are based on short-term actions and everyone wants to see quick results through decisive changes. **It's easy to do the wrong thing… quickly!**

Therefore, we need some strong, simple, and consistent beliefs and tools to slow us down and give us confidence to address the small and soft issues that may have little short-term positive bottom-line impact, but often turn out to be a matter of life or death from the customer's point of view in the long term.

Principles

Biologically, we are animals: yet we are animals with the ability to rise above our basic animal instincts and use our unique human capacity to reason and think logically and objectively.

Our animal instincts are the ones that can provoke us into taking short-term actions, driven by our 'fight or flight system', the basic animalistic part of our brain, to get the sale. The fight or flight response is constantly triggered, both by the internal pressure to meet our goals and targets (the survival instinct), and by the thrill of the challenge of getting the sale (the fighting instinct).

In this situation we do not employ the deeper cognitive thinking part of our brain (where we find our conscience, values and principles), and we very often find ourselves violating our deepest principles and upsetting the very people who we need to be loyal to us, by taking short-term fight or flight actions.

So, in order to combat this massively strong animal instinct (and, let's face it we all get hijacked by it from time to time ... and some significantly more frequently than that), we need clear, published, and uncompromisingly supported organisational, team and individual mission, systems and tools, founded on long-term principles and goals, to keep us on the straight and narrow path. These principles, systems, and tools also need obsessive and uncompromising measures to make sure that all are continually held accountable to them.

Of course, this is easy to say but hard to do. It can also take a long time: it's slow selling. **If it was fast and easy then everyone would already be doing it** ... and, you don't need us to tell you this is usually not the case!

A holistic approach

In effect, we need therefore to adopt a holistic approach to each and every interaction we have with future, present, and past customers. This needs to be principle driven, systemically aligned, and behaviourally measured, in order to ensure that it is balanced, consistent, and supported by all.

Four aspects

This approach should include the following four aspects:

1. Attraction
2. Delight
3. Loyalty
4. Reputation

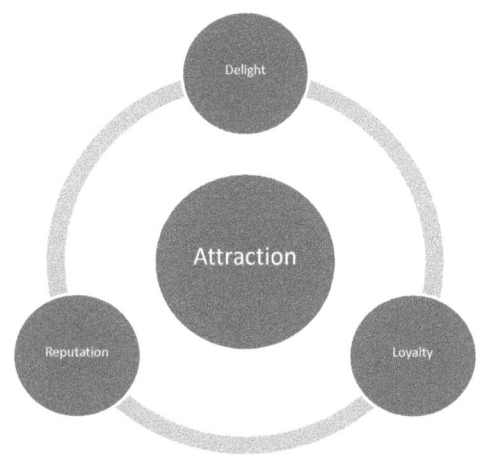

Likewise, we will suggest that in all businesses, everything should be driven through four principles that are aligned with these aspects.

1. Mission
2. Emotion
3. Action
4. Measure

We will suggest that every organisation, team, and individual, needs a **mission** that is based on constantly attracting the best people to work with them and to get queues of people wanting to do business with them.

The **emotion** we should aim to generate around us should be one of consistently delighting the customer – internal and external – through every step of every process, so they want to be loyal to us and rave about us, whether they do business with us today or not.

Our **actions** should be aligned with this mission and emotion, and should deliver consistent focus on inspiring loyalty and enthusiasm from everyone we come into contact with … no exceptions!

And our **measures** should start with our reputation and feedback on how well we have delivered the above intentions and actions. This should become, over time, the key lead measure that will provide the best possible results for the long term.

Then and only then will the profits flow: fully, abundantly, consistently, and sustainably.

This book is not about making sales and profits. **This book is about making full, abundant, consistent, sustainable, and rewarding long-term sales and profits.**

We perhaps can call this the state of being 'remarkable'. This term has a double meaning that is entirely aligned with this type of thinking and our aim in this book is to show you how to make your customer facing systems 'remarkable', so that you get queues of people wanting to buy from you, buying all they can from you, remaining fiercely loyal and raving about you to their friends.

These are the keys to 'selling'.

Balanced scorecard

The above four aspects can be effectively demonstrated by using a balanced scorecard that looks a bit like the diagrams above.

But remember, this is a balanced scorecard that means every aspect must be equally balanced. Any imbalance will result in significant underperformance in all areas. It's like the four wheels on your car, if one is misaligned, all four tyres will wear down significantly quicker.

The real problem

The real problem often is that due to pressure from shareholders and short-term targets, 90% of effort often goes into customer attraction and the remaining 10% gets shared, in a bun fight, between the others.

In traditional selling, customer attraction is seen not only as the number one focus, but also as an action of investment, with the other three aspects seen as very much of secondary importance and as an action of cost by the bean counters.

(And we all know that lots of money can be spent on investment, but costs always need to be minimised!).

The results are predictable, and seen all around us ... with brands rising quickly through high impact promotional activity and then falling away into the dust, with suppliers continually struggling to retain customers and ending up resorting to unsustainable special offers, and with organisations and individuals constantly struggling and often failing to keep up with the competition, achieve sustainable targets, and produce consistent profits.

An answer

An answer to all these issues is at the same time blindingly simple, and startlingly hard to apply.

If it wasn't, you'd see world-class levels of customer engagement, reputation, and loyalty all around you and marketing and advertising would become a very barren occupation.

Instead, we see ever-increasing levels of marketing and advertising chasing ever-lower levels of customer attention and loyalty.

Surely it's time to slow down, focus on common sense principles from start to finish throughout the sales process and, by doing this, **get customers queuing up to buy from you, buying all they can from you, becoming fiercely loyal, and raving about you behind your back?**

The beliefs, attitudes, skills, tools, and measures to make this actually happen for you in all your sales processes is what you will get from this book.

Thank you for buying it and we hope that you get massive value from it.

The Slow Sellers' Association

If you like the ideas in this book, we invite you to check out the 'Slow Sellers Association'.

Here you will find training resources, videos, tips, backup material, forums and Q&A sessions.

It's designed to be a simple, easy to use, helpful resource for individuals, managers and leaders everywhere who want help and support to stick with doing the right thing and getting customers lining up to do business with them.

www.slow-sellers.org

Preface

This book is different

This book is not directly about 'how to sell': **'Slow Selling' is about how to do things right, consistently, and how to continually improve them so that phenomenal levels of sales come automatically and persistently for the long-term.**

'Slow Selling' is also about how to get great levels of sales whilst also building remarkable levels of client happiness, loyalty, reputation, and referrals.

Sounds too good to be true? Well, in a nutshell, we guarantee it: if you read this book and implement the ideas in it and you don't see these kinds of results, please send it back for a full refund and an apology for wasting your time from the authors.

A Confession

We are not 'sales experts', we haven't read acres of print on 'sales', nor have we been 'trained by the leading sales organisations in the world'.

We would instead classify ourselves as specialists in customer loyalty, reputation and referrals ... so what makes us anyone worth listening to on the subject of 'sales'?

We have read and studied enough on sales to understand one thing above all else:
- The overwhelming focus of 'sales' systems are one sided and subconsciously based on a 'win-don't care' mindset.

When we study these approaches, we are often left with an overwhelming feeling of nausea: this is not a holistic and sensible long-term approach. It seems to us that these ideas focus on achieving a 'win' for the seller in the short term, with little or no attention to the long-term relationship or reputation.

'Traditional' sales processes focus on short term wins at the expense of the long term.

The problem is that these approaches have worked well in the world before two-way mass communication ... and are hard wired into organisations and individuals across the world, both emotionally and biologically: they are hugely tough to shift.

The issue is that they must be shifted in a world where your business is transparent and customers can talk about you, behind your back, without your knowledge or ability to moderate them, at the speed of light. This is the world we now live in, and the quicker we all wake up and recognise this, the better off we'll all be.

This is our take on this situation, and our attempt to help redress the balance and bring us back to a saner, kinder, more joyous and much more rewarding world ...

So, who is it for?

This book is for you if you are a business owner, leader, or manager who is struggling or confused or frustrated at not being able to get the results you want consistently and continually.

It is also for you if you are anyone wanting to sell anything a little bit easier, without sacrificing either your integrity or your margin.

Or are you simply struggling in your role against ever fiercer and more unpredictable competition, perhaps coming from the other side of the world?

Sometimes does everything seem a little bit like 'wading through mud' to get the results you crave?

Are you perhaps:
- A Business Owner who struggles to get high levels of engagement from your team?
- A Leader who gets frustrated that you cannot rely on your systems to produce consistent growth and consistent remarkable levels of reputation and customer loyalty?
- A Manager who is struggling to consistently motivate people to top levels of performance and feel that you have to be on people's backs, and double checking all the time?
- Someone in any role who is struggling to innovate and keep up with worldwide competition?
- Frustrated by the unfairness of customer reviews, and the unpredictability of online reputation?
- A Manager who needs to ensure that all your people perform to and above a certain standard in order to stop them (and you) being fired?

In a nutshell: **are you someone who is responsible for delivering consistent and continually improving sales results,**

whilst also developing remarkable levels of customer loyalty, in a world of ever tighter margins and ever fewer resources?

Yes? Of course you are … after all, 'selling' just means 'getting the results we want' in any given situation – we are all 'salespeople' in many different roles every day.

Then this book is for you … and the key message is:

In a world of frantic haste and cut-throat competition, the long-term winners slow down, get it right and build houses of concrete, not houses of cards.

How this book works

This book is designed to help you as follows:

1. Short and snappy points that you can dip in and out of (we've all got too much info!).
2. **Easy** to either read through to get the whole picture or take sections at random.
3. Diagrams and drawings to make points clear and memorable (for those of us who remember pictures better than words).
4. And we've added useful case studies (sparing names and blushes in many cases for professional reasons) with action plan suggestions for you.
5. 'Slow tips' to make simple, powerful points clear: so you can take this one step at a time.
6. Backed up by online support. You can contact us at any time for extra clarification or to ask for tailored support: all our contact details can be found at www.slow-selling.org .

Please of course remember, Rome wasn't built in a day: so don't try and do everything at once: take it slowly, get it right little by little, and be happy with progress and small victories: that's the best way to get large (and truly sustainable) victories over the long run.

We teach this idea as 'Go the Extra Inch'.

So, relax, enjoy it and go for it!

Note: in the book we will use the shorthand words for expediency:

- 'Product' as a shorthand term for any product or service that you want to sell, no matter what format it is in.
- 'Sell' as a shorthand term for getting what you want whether you sell it in a traditional way or not.
- 'Organisation' as a shorthand term for organisation, business, team or individual, whether large or small, public or private, profit making or non-profit making .
- We shall use the term 'speedy selling' as the opposite of 'slow selling': taken in this book to mean the selling ideas and processes of the 'old world' ... more on this later!

Please also note:
- Many of the examples and ideas are made extreme in order to make the points clearly: don't get too concerned about this, the emphasis is there to make the comparison clear and the learning easier. Don't get tempted to say 'that's a bit extreme, we're not really like that', but instead focus on the different approach and mindset set out in the 'slow selling countertype', in order to understand, learn from and apply this learning to your (probably less extreme) situation!
- Also, the case studies shown are often based on personal experience over the 20+ years we have been working with this material: they are true for the Author or the Author's associates: this doesn't mean to say they are necessarily universally true or are still true at the time you are reading this! Don't worry about this, just learn from the example and work on applying the principles to your organisation.

Part 1:

Introduction and Background

You need to **forget almost everything you learnt about sales over the past 300 years.** They were built in the 'one-way mass communication' world.

This world no longer exists.

Your customer is empowered with unlimited knowledge, can shop around the world, compare you with your competitors at the click of a button, share opinion with and listen to others talking about you behind your back, and is hugely distrustful of 'your marketing' as they've been misled and mis-sold for far too long.

Get it wrong and they'll screw you.

… and there's nothing you can do about it …

… except to 'be remarkable', consistently and continually in the first place!

But, in reality, can you get always 'be remarkable' consistently and continually?

No, of course not. However: here's the really good news:

If you put the slow selling processes in place, the customer will respond with trust and loyalty, and will promote you as remarkable person or organisation to do business with. This will allow you to make the odd mistake without being crucified, and to continually learn, develop and innovate so that your success is long term or and consistent.

In a nutshell, the world has changed forever: the 'normal' rules of sales and marketing no longer apply, and the process of selling has been turned on its head. **You can either stick to the old rules and watch yourself slowly and steadily be crucified, or you can change your systems, align yourself with the new rules and a new world, and watch your results slowly and steadily become remarkable.**

Your choice…

The key start point:
Background

What is 'Selling'?

Selling is the world's second oldest profession … often disguised as the first.

Selling is at its heart a noble profession that is there to:

- Get the right products to the right people in the right place at the right time.
- Drive continual innovation and improvement.
- Help people get what they need in order to be successful and happy in their lives.
- Get results!

But a terrible thing has happened to this noble profession over the last 300 years or so: as mechanisation and one-way mass media has dominated the world of commerce: this world of plenty and over supply, where organisations have called for **continual growth at all costs**, has meant that they have got exactly that: growth at the cost of 'remarkability' and 'sustainability'.

Sellers and marketers have had to become more and more devious and persuasive to shift the volume. This in turn has severely warped the world of selling to such an extent where it has almost become a dirty word.

This shows up in behaviours (from both individuals and organisations) such as:

- Quick fix 'selling techniques' continually promoted and trained ('catching butterflies while the elephants are escaping').
- Marketing that over promises and under delivers (dressing up mutton as lamb).
- Processes aimed at jam today at almost all costs ... and we'll worry about tomorrow if and when we get there ('killing the goose that lays the golden egg').
- The aim of 'making sales and profit target this quarter' driving all process and behaviour (while customer experience, reputation and loyalty go out of the window).
- A continual cycle of MDs and Sales Managers cajoling, threatening and demanding in ever more desperate attempts to meet targets. ('banging a drum no one can hear').
- Sales training coaching and training to embed new 'sales processes', or continuous reorganisation and rebranding ('rearranging deckchairs on the Titanic').

Indeed, in many organisations, this warped belief in 'how to sell' and 'what the shareholders want us to do', has made it almost impossible for individuals to do the right thing: resulting in

- Dysfunctional behaviour becoming the norm.
- Massive levels of stress, disengagement and job dissatisfaction becoming rife.
- Huge levels of customer ambivalence, resulting in continual costly and annoying switching.
- Underperformance against targets.
- Marketing having to become more and more devious or desperate.

And at extreme levels, fraud and cheating becoming standard.

Gallup's recent "State of the American workplace" survey of 195,000 employees reveals that only 33% of employees were actively engaged with their employment. The rest are either actively disengaged (16%) or neither one nor the other (in neutral). In his foreword to the survey Gallup's CEO Jim Clifton urges executives to address these results by committing to changing the culture from "command and control to one of high development and coaching conversations." As we'll see later in the book, this is a massive challenge.

The survey goes on to conclude that only 21% of employees strongly agree that their performance is managed in a way that motivates them to do outstanding work. Clifton goes on to conclude that:

"Employees feel rather indifferent about their job and the work they are being asked to do. Organizations are not giving them compelling reasons to stay, so it should come as no surprise that most employees (91%) say the last time they changed jobs, they left their company to do so."

Michael Brown: 'My Job isn't working'
https://myjobisntworking.com/

And...

the world has now changed.

The Internet and Social Media have radically transformed the way that information is distributed.

We are now in an age of organisational transparency, two-way mass communication, worldwide whistle blowing and customer empowerment via online reviews and social media.

To continue to act in the old dysfunctional ways of the industrialised mass market and one-way mass media, in a world that is now driven by global innovation and two-way mass media is madness. This 'brave new world' calls urgently for a return to the traditional values of selling, such as:

- Unconditional trust.
- Systems obsessively focused on customer reputation and loyalty.
- Customer engagement through feedback and collaboration.

This is the new approach to selling ... and it's also a return to the old traditional values of customer reputation and loyalty ... so, instead of the previous dysfunctional aim to:

'Sell as much as you can, as quickly as you can'

(through marketing and selling tricks and 'quick result techniques'), the new way to REALLY sell as much as you can, as quickly as you can ... for the LONG TERM, is what we call:

'Slow Selling'.

This book explains what this means, and how to implement this approach across all your activities.

If you like the sound of this so far, then we think you'll love the ideas we put forward.

Slow Tip:

Build a short 'Slow Down, Reflect and Think' time before and after every important meeting
Use a weekly plan to ensure you stick to what's important for you and your team(s).

We are social animals

We are social animals, **and one thing that social animals should NEVER speed up is attraction and relationship building with each other**: in other words, 'SELLING'.

- Customers hate email spam: yet most internet marketing advocates 'more exposure of the brand'.
- Customers turn off Internet ads, and desert platforms that are covered with them: yet organisations still continually pay for them.
- Customers hate interruptions: yet 'interruption marketing' is seen as a 'good thing' to do.
- Customers crave genuine trust and ease of doing business above everything else: yet marketing usually derides this and rarely invests in it, going instead for the 'quick fix'.

The major change in communication

We have come from a world of one-way mass communication where 'large' organisations could dominate their market though media domination, and brands could sleepwalk consumers into eschewing them. But today we're in a different world, where customers can find out what they want for themselves, and share their opinions with the world at the touch of a button.

The age of 'push' marketing, short termism and 'speed selling' is over.

It's time to slow down, go back to common sense principles and build customer loyalty and trust for long term success.

If genuine social relationships really matter (and they do), then it's logical to suggest that any product that needs significant artificial promotion to stay successful can't be very good in reality, can it?

(Of course, nothing's THAT simple (and customers are driven by emotion, not logic): but hold on to the principle, and we'll explain the systems to make the principles work effectively for you, forever in a short while!).

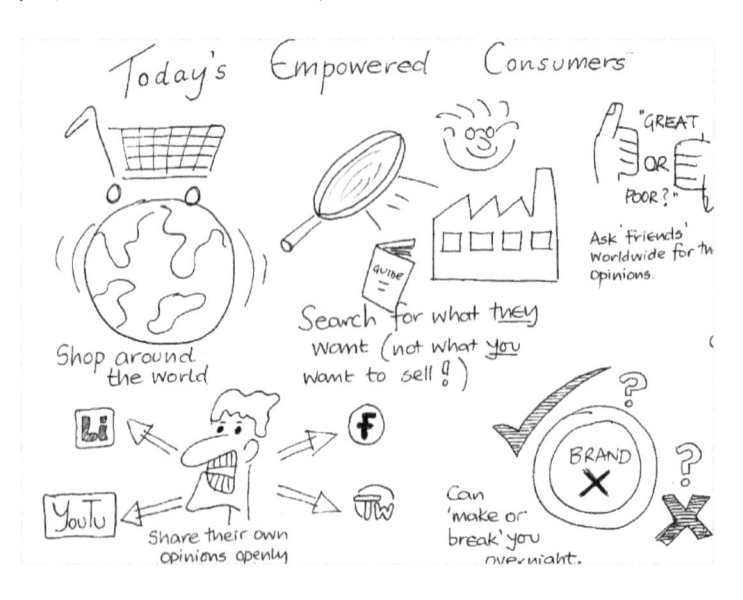

Slow Tip:

Examine your offer: try to always describe it in words that ideal customers would use about it: what would you want people to say about it behind your back?

Hunter / Gatherers

'Selling' as a profession has been honed and manipulated to give great results in a world driven by one-way mass communication.

This is, by necessity, a short-term 'get results today and we'll worry about tomorrow when we come to it' approach, and it has worked fine (provided the organisation kept pedalling!) in a world where demand outstripped supply and this 'one-way mass communication' environment meant that the organisation had more knowledge and power than the customer.

It also has the advantage of being perfectly aligned with our 'hunter/gatherer' nature, where the drive comes from our natural instinct, not only to hunt, but also to gather as much as possible as we can (to keep us from starving in the hard times that may lie ahead). This will, by necessity drive an understandable 'survival of the fittest' approach … and in the world of one-way marketing dominated mass communication, this wasn't too much of a problem. A few enlightened organisations acted differently (Victorian organisations founded on Quaker principles being a good example of this), but, generally, the 'norm' has been to act in 'a hunter / gatherer way'.

And as mechanisation and globalisation of trade sped up the ability to make profits, and business owners became more and more remote from their customers, the more this type of behaviour has become systemised and institutionalised.

Indeed, it has worked so well and is so embedded in our nature, that it has become an all-powerful drive that people often struggle to escape.

But escape they must, and resist their baser animal instincts they must ... for we are now in a world where:

- Supply outstrips demand.
- Enlightenment, customer awakening and demand for 'genuine value' is the norm.
- Customers have more knowledge and power than the organisation.
- And reputation, both good and bad, can be spread worldwide at the speed of light.
- The true environmental impact of Industrial hunter/gathering is becoming apparent and repulsive to many.

And in this brave new world, sticking to 'hunter / gatherer' ways of 'selling' and not paying the price of behaving more intelligently than our basic animal instincts will land us in the soup, one way or another, sooner or later. It's only a question of time ...

This applies to organisations as much as it does to individuals.

It's time to rise above our animal instincts, slow down and get it right for the long term.

Slow Down!

If you 'get' what we've stated above you need to do a number of things in order to escape from the morass of mundanity and start on the ladder of remarkability.

success!

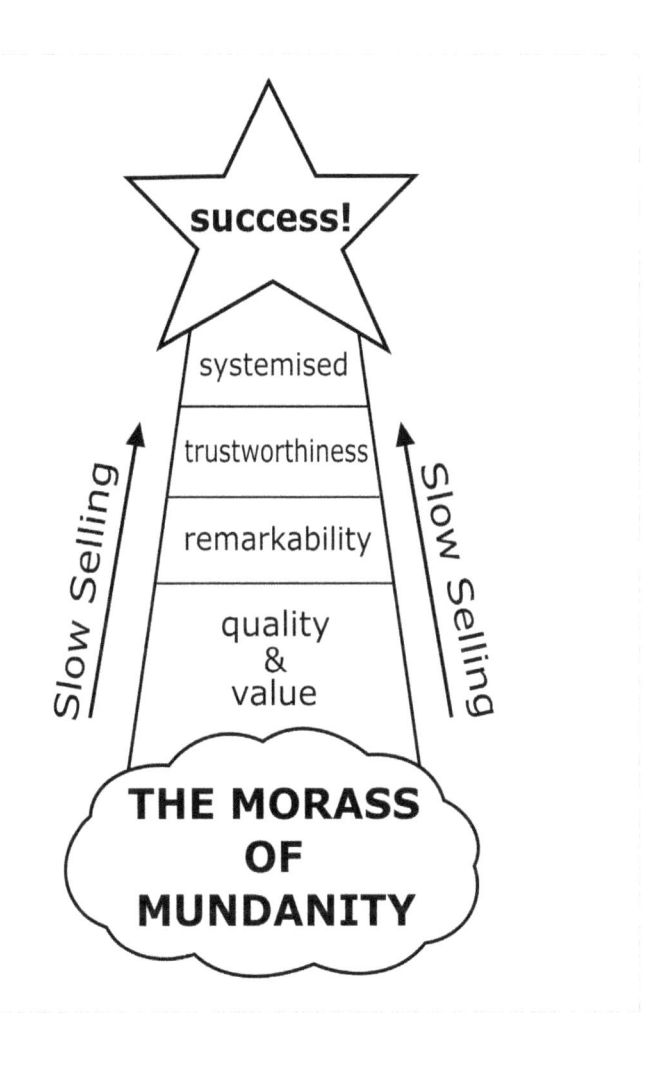

| systemised |
| trustworthiness |
| remarkability |
| quality & value |

Slow Selling ↑   Slow Selling ↑

THE MORASS OF MUNDANITY

Slow Tip:

Remember: quality and remarkability take time: slow down and start developing more effective habits one step at a time.
- It took Amazon 18 years as a Public Company to catch WalMart in market cap ... but only 2 years to more than double it
- Google waited and slowly developed their systems for over 8 years before feeling they were 'good enough' to go public

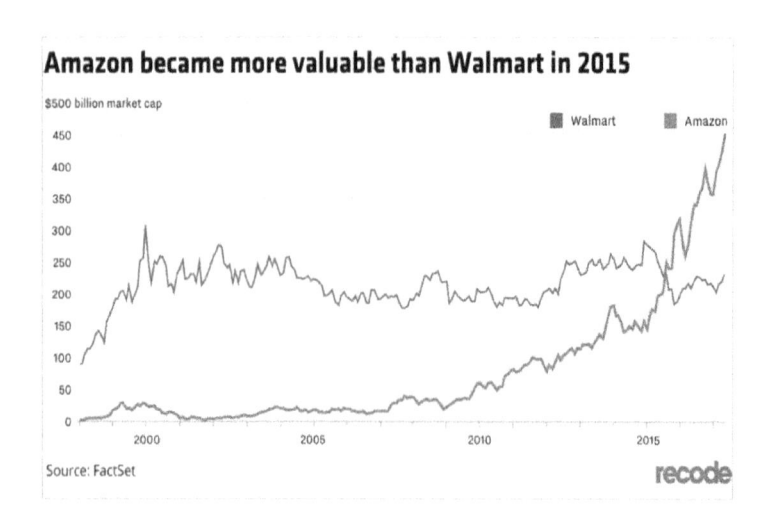

Amazon became more valuable than Walmart in 2015

Source: FactSet

Here's a few pointers:

1. **Learn and grow** (you're doing this by reading this book): keep it up!
2. **Assess your current situation:** will it let you flourish in this more enlightened world or not? If so, continue to work on yourself every week, step by step, and find others in your organisation who can help you. If not, perhaps you could consider changing your situation?

3. **Actively seek feedback as a new habit**, both individually and organisationally: you may think you're doing the 'right thing' but the only person who can tell you for sure is the person you're doing it to!
4. **Keep developing and questioning**: start using the ideas in this book one by one: when things go well, ask *'How could I make them go even better in the future?'* When things go badly, ask *'What can I learn from this to help me improve and grow?'*
5. Remember the Buddhist proverb: '**when the pupil is ready, the teacher appears**'.

And if you reject what we're saying, stop reading this book and instead go online to search for 'sales techniques' and 'quick fixes' …

Slow Tip:

Sharpen the Saw: Make a personal commitment to embrace continual growth and learning: use a weekly plan to make this actually happen.

Every quarter, start with a blank slate and reassess you and your market: where are we? What has changed? What do we know? What do we need to know that we don't? where do we want to be in 3 months time?

Every customer is a long-term high value one in the customer empowered world

Ok, so there are a lot of objections and questions to this 'Slow-Selling' approach. Not least of which is:

- 'I only make a small amount per transaction, how on earth can I afford to spend high value quality time and effort on this, I barely break even at the moment'

It's much easier to agree that 'Slow-Selling' makes huge amounts of sense for B2B selling and high value situations, but what about low-value, high volume situations?

Remember the story of the Hare and the Tortoise: could there be some similarities?

Let's just consider: here's a simple assessment of what 'Slow-Selling' perhaps can do. If you make $10 profit on every transaction and have 1000 transactions a week (to make the maths simple), you'll make $520,000 per year. Here's a simple proposal of what 'Slow-Selling' can and will do for you (all other things being equal for the sake of clarity on this point).

'Slow-Selling' enables you to	Which means that your profit per transaction is	Number of weekly transactions	Change in weekly costs	Annual profit
Put price up by 10%	$11	1000	0	$575,000
Sell up another product to 20% of customers	$10	1200	0	$624,000
Get a 20% referral rate	$10	1200	0	$624,000
Increase velocity of sales over the long term	$10	1500	0	$780,000
If all the above happen	$11	1900	0	$1,086,800

Slow Tip:

Do this 'back of an envelope' exercise using real numbers in your market.

Check it's realistic

Then use it as the basis of your strategy going forward

Now, of course, you aren't gullible, you know that we've just plucked the above figures out of the air. And you know that nothing's ever that simple. And, let's face it, it will cost you extra to be a 'Slow-Seller'. You may well need a few more people and you may well need to invest (slowly) in higher quality and more remarkable systems.

But, here's the true learning from the above exercise:

- In reality, for low value, high volume goods or services, once you get it right your sales can explode: the above figures are probably ridiculously conservative!
- For lower volume, higher value products, the massive opportunity lies in margin, up selling, cross selling and referrals: this can multiply your bottom-line profit by significant amounts for relatively small amounts of investment in time and effort.
- On top of this, there's the negative aspect to consider. If you don't do it properly, someone else probably will and it's easy to consider that you could lose all your 'existing customers' overnight. So perhaps you have to start doing this just to stay alive … after all your 'existing customers' don't belong to you: they're just using your services because they haven't found anything better yet. Just consider how slowly 'traditional' retailers responded to the advent of Amazon, or hotels to TripAdvisor.

- This shows that you can easily consider investing a good % of your marketing budget into 'Slow-Selling' for long term results, as long as you do your homework first (which usually involves understanding the needs of your customers more closely through proper feedback processes as a starting point).

> Remember: **'your' customers don't 'belong' to you**: slow down and spend time developing systems and behaviours that they will passionately WANT to be loyal to!
>
> - It takes 20 years to build a reputation and 5 minutes to lose it (Warren Buffet)
> - Your brand is what people say about you behind your back (Jeff Bezos: CEO of Amazon)
> - Over 80% of 'satisfied' customers won't use your brand next time (Source: Coca Cola)

Which means that

Perhaps you may need a totally new approach and systems for your selling: here's where you need to be in the very near future (or preferably now):

1. **Our core belief could be:** 'We're not here to sell stuff, we're here to do something so well that people can't wait to buy our stuff (and also rave about us behind our backs)'.
2. **Our systems could be filtered slowly and methodically** one by one through the 'Customers' REAL Needs':
   a. **TRUST:** do our systems engender uncompromising trust?
      i. Competence: do we know our market, our customer's market, and all the options that are open to the customer? Do we keep rigorously up to date with this?

ii. Character: do we have sound character (driven by rule one) and do we ensure we remain loyal to this in all we do, through thick and thin, no matter how dysfunctional and difficult the market around us becomes?
b. **EASIER / BETTER LIFE:** do we aim to make our customer's life easier or better in all we do?
    i. Indirect: do we design all our processes around making this happen?
    ii. Direct: do we practise this in all our actions?
c. **ATTENTION:** do we genuinely care … and go out of our way to demonstrate this?
    i. Physically: in all our physical actions and processes?
    ii. Emotionally: in the way we do all the above: do we act in a way that demonstrates genuine care for the other party … whether they ae a paying customer or not? Are we 'remarkable' for the right reasons?

T E A
trust   easier   attention
        better
        life

THE CUSTOMER'S REAL NEEDS

3. **We have rigorous accountability and continual improvement processes.** Every day, every week and every month we have sacrosanct processes to help us stay in touch with what's really happening and continually improve all we do and how we do it, step by step. All our people are focused, committed and motivated and held rigorously accountable through

reviews and systems. These systems produce a cadence of continual improvement and development.

4. **We have simple and powerful lead measures,** measuring the actions that produce the results. These are publicly shown and owned by all the team because we have a clear and compelling scoreboard and are held rigorously accountable to performance through step 3 above. We also have lag measures but we know that these only go in the right direction because of our focused rigorous attention to the lead measures.

5. All the above is backed up and supported **by top quality professional customer feedback and engagement systems** ... we are 'Investors in Feedback'.

6. We have monthly, quarterly and annual re-examination and macro **improvement systems** to keep reviewing and improving all the above.

7. We have **access to experts** in these key fields outside our organisation who work with us in a hands-off manner to keep us on track (because we know how hard it is to stay on course).

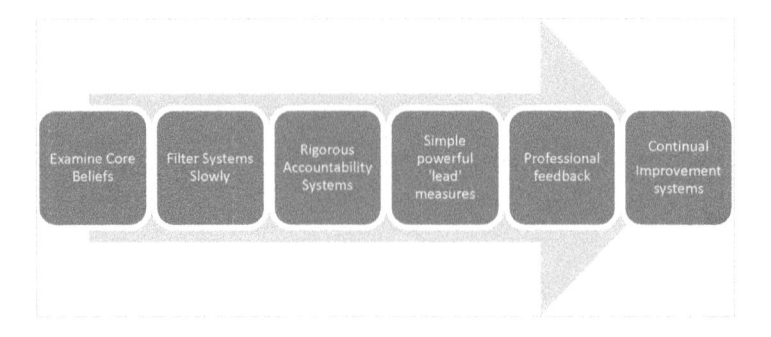

Examine Core Beliefs → Filter Systems Slowly → Rigorous Accountability Systems → Simple powerful 'lead' measures → Professional feedback → Continual Improvement systems

Now your next steps are to examine where your biggest gaps seem to be, and then work on these in order of priority, one at a time.

The material and ideas in this book will help you: keep reading, share with colleagues, act in small steps, keep reviewing and gathering feedback and then you'll have ideas on how to close the gaps.

Start with Why: In his wonderful book 'Start with Why', Simon Sinek makes the point that, until people are clear on, and support, the 'why' we are doing something, they cannot and will not be passionately committed to it. Indeed, quite the opposite will be true: they will be far more likely to be demotivated and disillusioned … (does that ring any bells?).

And remember:
- To make more profit, or
- To be the biggest

Are not motivational 'whys' in 99% of people's books …!

So: **WHY bother** with 'Slow Selling' and trying to be 'remarkable' for the right reasons?

That's up to you to decide, based on your beliefs, motivations and principles: but, here's our view for what it's worth.

Quite apart from the undeniable fact that 'Slow Selling' makes you a lot more money over the long term, in our opinion it has the following benefits:
- It's much more enjoyable
- It adds value to both parties
- It's fulfilling
- We are a species sharing an existence our very survival depends on cooperation and mutual benefit … period!

'Start with Why' by Simon Sinek: https://startwithwhy.com/

Slow Tip:

Start with 'Why?'

The problem with 'traditional selling'

In a nutshell the problem with 'traditional selling' is that it's 'frightening'.

- Fear of not getting the result we want.
- Fear of wasting time and effort.
- Fear of feeling bad.
- Fear of not satisfying the ego.
- Fear of 'losing'.
- Fear of my boss / targets / job security.

And when fear kicks in, it triggers our 'Fight or Flight' system. We then lose the ability to keep calm and think properly, and stress kicks in.

And the fear is also there in the mind of the customer, resulting in the same biological problems happening:

Slow Tip:

Talk about 'fear' and 'fears' with your people.
Identify where they are, who has them, where they kick in and what the consequences are.
Then start to address them, step by step.

- Fear of ignorance / being ripped off.
- Fear of failure / looking stupid / buyer's remorse.
- Fear of over spending.
- Fear of getting the wrong thing / having unnecessary aggro.
- Fear of not satisfying the ego.
- Fear of my boss / my targets / not achieving my goals.

And the result of all this is:
- Hyped up promises from the seller.
- Unnecessary barriers from the buyer.
- Untruths and posturing from both sides.
- Broken promises and false aspirations.

In other words: a great recipe for chaos, stress and serious under performance on both sides.

And the natural response to this (driven by the 'fight or flight response) is: **Go faster!**

Perhaps it's time to consider going slower?

'Slow Selling' is the '3rd Alternative'!

When you slow down, stop trying to 'push sell' and focus all your systems and behaviour on building trust, making the potential customer's life easier and showing that you genuinely care and want to 'get it right', then the customer relaxes and the whole process becomes easier, quicker and much more effective. And 'fight or flight' doesn't get a look in at all.

We call this 'The 3rd Alternative' to 'Fight or Flight'.

> For more information on **'The 3rd Alternative'** please see Stephen Covey's wonderful book on the subject.
>
> *http://www.the3rdalternative.com/*

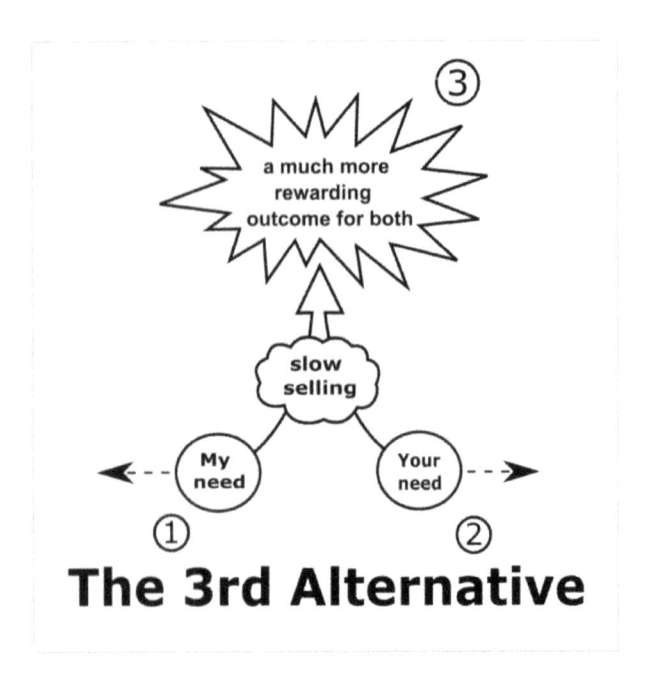

The 3rd Alternative

There are 5 outcomes to a Sales Process (and not all of them are great!)

In most 'traditional' sales strategies, the focus is usually on 'getting a sale'.

But this is far too simplistic … and in today's world of instant online reviews and the empowered customer, it's downright dangerous. In fact, there are five outcomes to a sales process, and they ALL need to be considered, trained and considered in order to get GREAT long term sales results.

This is so much more than just 'hitting target this week'!

Let's look at them in turn, from worst to best:
1. 'I'll come back to you': this is called a **'no decision'**: where the customer hasn't made a decision, or has made one but hasn't told you! The output of this is usually monumental time-wasting and unnecessary time, cost and aggro.
    - The main reason for this outcome is: you haven't done your job properly: the customer hasn't trusted you enough to keep discussing with you until they were confident to say either 'yes' or 'no'. OR they don't trust you enough to tell you what they're REALLY thinking.
2. **'Yes' for the wrong reasons**: this is where you get the sale, but for the 'wrong' reasons. 'So what's wrong with this? I've got the sale … happy days!' you may ask. Well yes, that may be the case if you describe 'happy days' as:
    - High levels of complaints and returns.
    - High levels of poor online reviews.
    - Business success dependent more and more on deals, marketing push and 'special offers'.
3. **'No' for the wrong reasons**: this is where you don't get the sale, but you could have: you would have been the best supplier for the job, but you weren't able to build enough rapport and get the customer to trust you enough for them to understand the full nature of their

need, the market, and how you could be the best long term solution for them.
4. **'No' for the right reasons**: many sales managers would like to rip our tongue out for this, but a 'no' for the right reasons is a 'good' outcome.
    - This is where you've built a great relationship with the customer, and have together agreed that, all things considered, your solution isn't the best fit for the client, and you help them instead by pointing them in other directions.
5. If you do your selling properly, although this customer won't use you today, when and if their need changes, they'll come back to you. In the meantime, they'll recommend you, and they might well use your services anyway (fully aware that you're not a 100% fit) because you're so helpful and trustworthy … and, by the way, no matter what your manager tells you, you can NEVER sell something to everyone … you'll NEVER get 100% success rate: it's blindingly obvious common sense, so stop worrying about it, get rid of the fear and instead just ENSURE all your 'No's are gained for the right reasons! And of course, the 'best' outcome is always a **'yes' for the 'right' reasons**: this is where you not only get the sale today, but you also get great levels of customer happiness, loyalty and reputation: a true win/win!

So, we need to make sure that we get none of items 1,2 and 3 and all of items 4 and 5.

Slow Tip:

- Teach 'The 5 outcomes to a sales process' to all.
- Put systems in place to get you to outcomes 4 or 5 in all cases.
- Agree follow up processes for when people get it wrong.
- This will start to seriously reduce any fear.

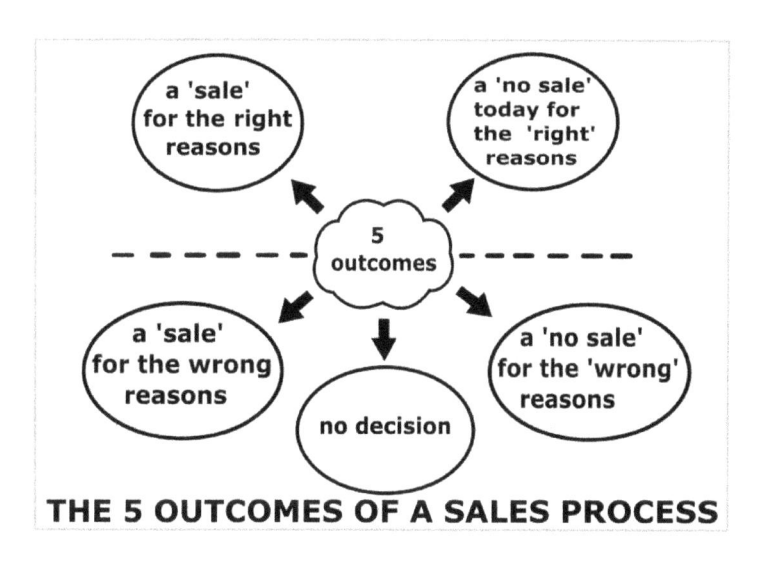

THE 5 OUTCOMES OF A SALES PROCESS

- a 'sale' for the right reasons
- a 'no sale' today for the 'right' reasons
- a 'sale' for the wrong reasons
- no decision
- a 'no sale' for the 'wrong' reasons

ABC changes to ABH

There's a wonderful 'narrow mindset' corker of a principle in 'traditional selling' and its:

ALWAYS BE CLOSING

I.e. Make sure everything is designed and executed to 'close' the sale. (And for a wonderful demonstration of this mindset, please see the excellent film 'Glengarry, Glenross').

But, as you're smarter than that, and reading this book, I'm sure you'll be thinking by now:

'How stupid! This is the exact thing that customers hate and that will get us many sales for the wrong reasons! Thus destroying our reputation and loyalty!'

Yes, that's exactly right. And it also will:

- Destroy sales that you could have had for the right reasons (had you sold a little more slowly).
- Skyrocket the number of 'No Decisions' you'll get.
- Cause you to waste hours and hours on dead ends (because while you're 'always closing' the customer will be fighting you tooth and nail by 'always lying').

This shallow minded silliness (that worked OK in the age of one way mass communication) must now change in everything you do.

In a nutshell, we suggest that: **'Always be closing'**: changes to **'Always be helping'** (and the results will take care of themselves).

Slow Tip:

Make **'Always be helping'** your sales mantra that guides all process and behaviour.

ABH always be helping

beneficial
harmful

ABC always be closing

TRANSFORM YOUR SALES INTENT RISE TO THE CHALLENGE!

'Sellers' and 'Servers'

There is a curious belief in many Organisations that 'Sales' and 'Service' are separate areas of operation.

They are not, of course:
- 'Sales' without 'service' will drive you full speed into a brick wall.
- 'Service' without 'sales' will sink you.

So it's just as important to ensure those people in your Organisation who are primarily 'service' orientated, also are trained in slow selling, so that they develop confidence and skills in converting great service into extra sales, cross sales and up sales.

They are in the perfect situation to do this because they have started in the right place … but, so often, they are scared and nervous about the whole idea of 'selling'.

This, of course, needs to be done sensitively and carefully, and in today's world of global competition and high customer expectations … it needs to happen: consistently and continually.

You cannot afford any sellers not to be focused on service, nor can you afford any servers not to be focused on sales.

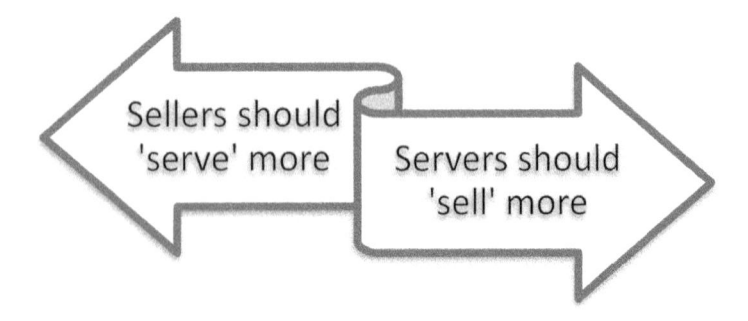

Sellers should 'serve' more ⇐ ⇒ Servers should 'sell' more

Slow Tip:

- Train servers to sell more and sellers to serve more.
- Develop joined up processes and skill sets
- Job share to gain understanding
- Measure and incentivise serving before selling (more on this later)

Part 2:
The Four Principles of Human Behaviour

The Four Principles of Human Behaviour

We all display four universal behavioural traits, regardless of our skills, personality, and appearance – they are the bedrock on which we build our lives, they influence all our results and an understanding of them is crucial to our understanding of what will make us successful or otherwise.

Indeed, the whole 'Slow Selling' sales process is built around their structure.

Indeed, in this new world of business transparency and customer empowerment, if you get these principles wrong, you're in much more trouble that you could possibly know…

Here's an explanation:

PEOPLE BEHAVE LIKE BEARS

beliefs
emotions
actions
results

BELIEFS, EMOTIONS, ACTIONS, RESULTS…… (B.E.A.R.s)

BELIEFS:
Everyone has a unique set of beliefs (derived from their background, upbringing, situation, education etc.).

EMOTIONS:
Their beliefs drive their emotions and their (usually) learned response to how they feel about anything that comes their way.

ACTIONS:
Which in turn guides what they will do in any given situation.

RESULTS
And these actions then give them their results which often are expected from belief stage (a 'self-fulfilling prophecy'), but occasionally not (a 'strange occurrence'). Our results tend therefore to reinforce our beliefs and emotions (and turn our actions into habits).

In general, our beliefs will determine the emotions actions and results in a circular system (what we believe generally comes true), reinforcing our original beliefs.

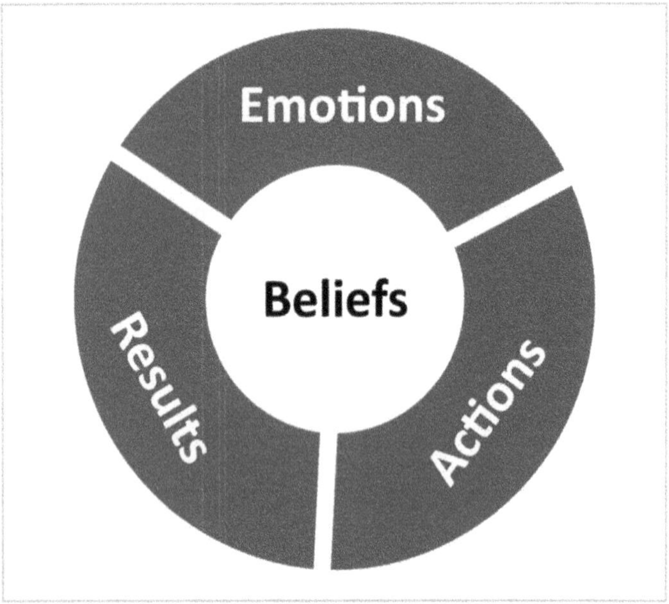
Emotions
Beliefs
Results
Actions

These four principles have led to many articles, papers and books, but for the purposes of this book, the thing that we need to understand is: **We need to accept these principles and work on all 4 areas simultaneously to get a balanced, sustainable and optimum long-term result.**

As the B.E.A.R. process is circular if we fail or rush one area we impact (mess up) the whole cycle, therefore let us explore each area in turn.

BELIEFS

Every one of us is unique, with unique background, upbringing, environment, experience and habits. Consequently, we have our own unique beliefs.

Beliefs influence our emotions, actions and results very strongly (we believe in the integrity of what we are trying to do). So, for long term success, we need to address our own and our team's thinking (belief in the organisation, its aims and direction), and work tirelessly to develop our customers' beliefs (that this is a genuine win/win partnership that brings mutual benefit).

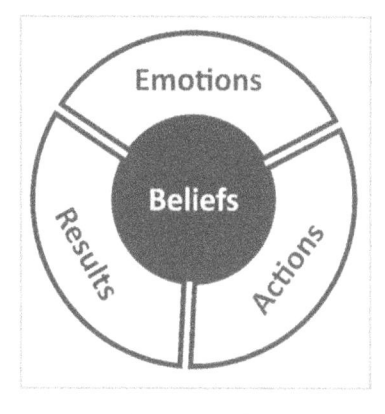

(And all this against a background of learned disinterest, mistrust and cynicism from these very people we seek to influence).

The key principles are:

    a. You can only get sales right for the long term if you genuinely believe 'The Golden Rule': Treat your customer as you'd like to be treated if you were them (in this situation). (And remember, if you manage others, your first customer is your team: apply these principles to your relationship with them first, then empower them (and hold them accountable) to do the same with your external customer).

    b. Develop a 'Customer Focused Mission': this is a short, simple, clear, empowering, and measurable guide to what your key belief is and what you'd like your customer to say or do behind your back (more detail on this later).

    c. Treat this as a 'compass' to guide all your stakeholder needs, mission, strategy, processes and behaviour.

d. No excuses: no 'I'll do that when times get better, but for now I need to make my target': it's all or nothing!

EMOTIONS

Our beliefs are the driving force behind our emotions, so, in order to be able to influence others' emotions (and 'sell') things properly), we need to figure out what REAL emotions are being driven by the beliefs of our customers in their 'hidden core'. Only then when we understand their emotions can we properly engage and sell to these customers effectively.

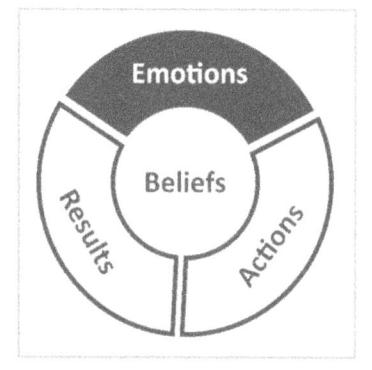

We call this 'The Customer's REAL needs'

Here are some of the questions that the sales system must address in order to engage the customer emotionally:

- Do we genuinely care about customers, or are they merely a means to an end?
- Do we go out of our way to make their lives easier?
- Are we genuinely trustworthy?
- Are we demonstrating clearly that we really value the customer, through our behaviour or is this just lip-service?
- How do we know what the REAL deep-down beliefs and emotions of our customer are?

Your customer knows better than you do (or indeed your sales director, M.D. or shareholders) what is right for them, and what will make them want to buy more from you, more often and become your chief advocate and promoter in their peer group, and that, ultimately is what you want, and what this SLOW-SELLING

SYSTEM is designed to achieve.

Only when the customers believe that we are both engaged on an emotional level will they truly trust us…. **people don't care how much you know until they know how much you care.**

The key principles are:

   a. Customers buy emotionally to satisfy physical needs and wants: spend a lot of time continually 'peeling the onion' to find out your customers' current and desired emotions: this will drive reputation and loyalty more than anything else.
   b. Remember the customers KEY emotional needs (they are simple and clear but their importance bears different weight depending on your product and situation). Remember them using the 'TEA' acronym:
      i. Trust
         1. Competence: do you get it right?
         2. Character: are you trustworthy?
      ii. Easier/better life
         1. Physically: your systems?
         2. Emotionally: your communication and behaviour?
      iii. Attention
         1. Direct: in all you do.
         2. Indirect: in all your systems.

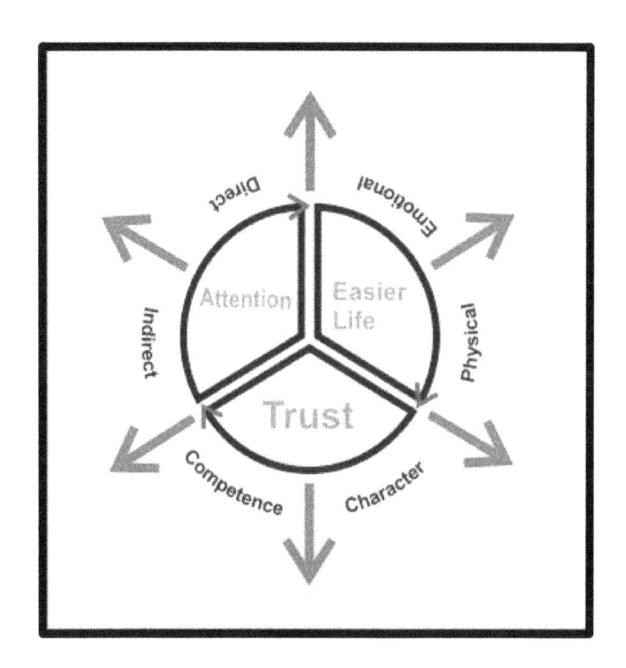

c. Treat this as a 'filter' to guide all your strategy, processes and behaviour.
d. Remember: any chain is only as strong as it's weakest link, and the world around you is always changing. Keep focusing and filtering, every week, using simple tools (which we will demonstrate later) to keep your chain strong.

ACTIONS

Knowledge is useless without action, so once you know and understand the beliefs and emotional driving forces behind your customer then you need to align the actions of your sales process, step by step, to address these.

You also need to take continual action, in small steps, to listen, evolve, improve, develop, build loyalty, build cross and up sales, and get referrals.
We call this 'Go the Extra Inch'.

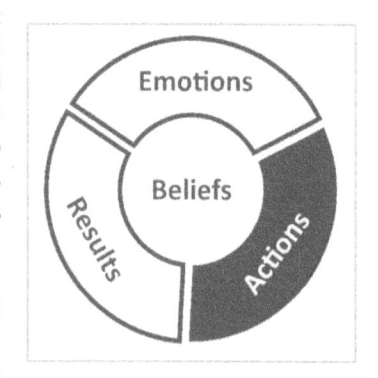

The key principles are:

a. Nothing stands still: if you're not continually taking action to move forward and get continually better, then, by default you're moving backwards and getting worse.
b. True progress that lasts and makes a measurable impact for the long term is always in small steps: there is no quick fix. All 'overnight successes' are the product of

years of hard graft and application of continual improvement in small steps (just ask any Olympic Athlete).
c. Focus on setting up and obsessively executing systems of continual development in 4 areas:
   i. People: getting the right people. Training and empowering them, developing them, holding them accountable, generating love for the job in them.
   ii. Process: continual innovation and evolution of all processes to make 'beautiful machines' based on continual feedback from, and in-depth listening to the internal and external customer.
   iii. Behaviour: the output of getting the above two right: then finding simple clear and compelling measures to continually influence behaviour for the better and for genuine win/win outcomes.
   iv. Relationship: continual development of the relationship with the customers so they become more loyal and want to tell all their friends about you.
      1. The way you do this will depend on the business you're in, but, in a nutshell, here's some guidance:
         a. The internal customer: clear job descriptions, empowerment and accountability, with continual reviews, 360-degree feedback and success sharing
         b. B2B relationships: continual development of a win/win relationship so your input helps them succeed in more and better ways.
         c. B2C 'significant' purchases: quality feedback and relationship building.

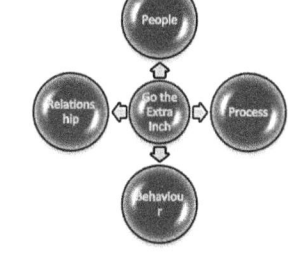

d. B2C 'basic' purchases: systemic feedback and system development to gain their enthusiastic loyalty.

We will examine this principle in more depth throughout in the book.

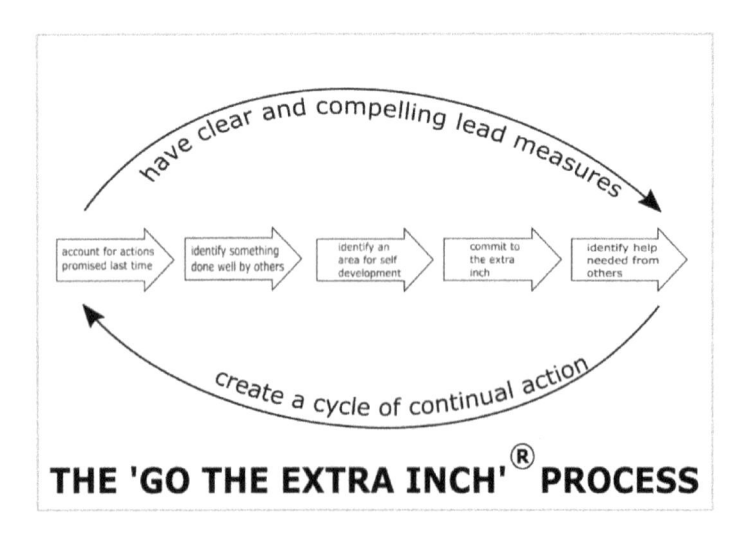

have clear and compelling lead measures

account for actions promised last time → identify something done well by others → identify an area for self development → commit to the extra inch → identify help needed from others

create a cycle of continual action

THE 'GO THE EXTRA INCH'® PROCESS

RESULTS

What gets measured gets done

For each action that you take, you will need a measure to know and understand how effective each step is and to help refine and improve all that is done.

These are called 'lead' measures: they are measures of activity or results that indicate what will happen in the future: a bit like a barometer or a weather forecast will predict what the weather will do in the future because of the measurements they have taken: these measures, combined with professional feedback, will help you achieve the results you want.

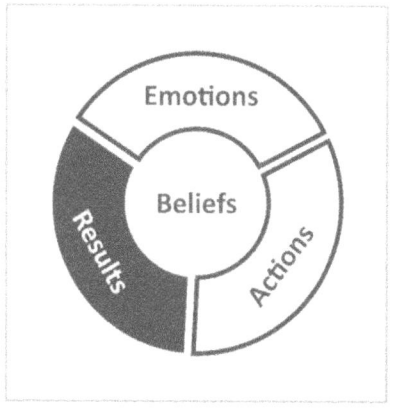

The key principles are:

a. What gets measured gets done.
b. If you can measure something, you can improve it: if you can't, you can't.
c. Find simple 'lead' measures of activities and outcomes that, if improved, are likely to result in higher levels of customer loyalty, reputation and referrals: if you focus on improving the right inputs, step by step, the outputs will correspondingly improve step by step.

d. Most measures in organisations are unbalanced: they are simply money (outputs or 'lag measures') focused. Create a balanced scorecard, with the 'lead' measures as the key activity drivers, then share success from the 'lag' measures.
e. Use your feedback and measures to find valuable and continual key information about vital areas in your business or team: motivation, empowerment, commitment, process, strategy and beliefs.
f. Innovate and evolve using the 'lead' measures and feedback to drive your 'Go the extra inch' processes.

Follow these B.E.A.R. Footprints and you will find that your SLOW-SELLING processes lead to:

- Reducing sales effort
- Increasing customer loyalty
- More direct referrals
- Building an excellent reputation
- Encouraging new ideas and products
- Increasing order size and frequency
- Innovating more effectively and efficiently
- Cutting unnecessary costs
- Stopping doing unprofitable things

And of course, SELLING MORE.

We will now use these 4 principles as a structure to examine current selling principles and ideas (described here as 'speedy selling') and the 'Slow Selling Countertype' to each one.

(Note: for detailed explanation and analysis of these 4 principles, and how they apply to all strategy, process and behaviour in your organisation, please see 'Great or Poor' by Guy Arnold ISBN: 9781852526931).

A Short Rant about Feedback

Feedback is NOT a 'customer satisfaction survey'!

Feedback is a customer focused, systematically organised ongoing professional system, to supercharge your continual improvement processes, inch by inch.

Done properly, it will do all that we've stated above.

Done improperly (and 95% of all 'feedback' and 'customer surveys' fall into this category), it will waste everyone's time, annoy your customers, provide inaccurate information and drive you mad.

We call this 'Chasing butterflies while the elephants are escaping'.

You MUST get this right: this is a complicated and delicate system that needs careful and continual attention. Done properly, it's supercharge your sales. Done badly, it'll be like wading through mud.

Please contact us for advice on where to go to get this done right if you're not sure.

investors in
feedback

For further information and guidance, we suggest you have a look at 'Investors in Feedback': www.investorsinfeedback.com
Rant over …

Slow Selling ... no matter what situation you're in

One last word before we move onto the meat of 'Slow Selling': you may not be the boss in your organisation, or even in your team or job. You might be thinking: "I would never be allowed to do this".

And you might be right ... for now.

But what about next month, next year or even the rest of your career?

We would suggest that if you're not directly in control of the systems and processes in your workplace, don't expect miracles: just because you like the ideas we put forward here, doesn't mean that anyone else will.

But, here's the good news:

This is YOUR life! You can do anything you want with it: so, if you're not in direct control, take direct control of what you personally CAN do. Improve all the tiny ways you can, and look continually for small opportunities to develop and change:

Small changes over time can have LARGE impacts.

SMALL CHANGES OVER TIME CAN HAVE LARGE IMPACTS

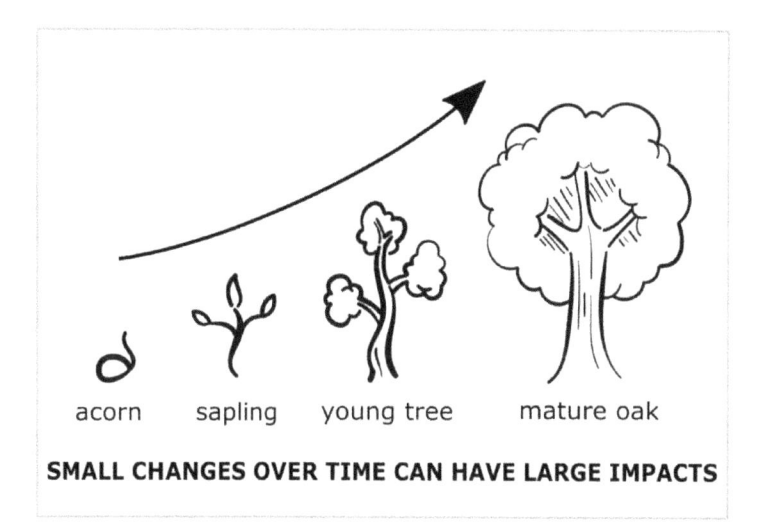

If you start using unilaterally some of the ideas we put forward here, then you may well see some of the following results:

- Your customers will become more loyal and want to buy more from you.
- You'll start getting excellent customer feedback.
- The actions you take will start to be noticed.
- Your results will steadily improve.
- You'll start rising in the sales rankings.

And, eventually, you'll either be noticed and promoted or your Organisation will start to ask you why you're doing so well compared to your peers, and what systems you think need to be changed.

And then you'll be truly succeeding in all senses of the word.

We call this: 'Slow Selling … no matter what situation you're in':

And we thoroughly recommend this as a life philosophy!

There are only 2 possible outcomes to this if you do it properly:

1. Either: the above scenarios will happen (you succeed over time).
2. Or: they won't …. In which case you now have a conundrum:
    a. Either: I stay and put up with it (not very attractive?).
    b. Or: now I'm a top performer I can start looking around for better opportunities with more enlightened Organisations (you succeed over time).

Slow Tip:

Whatever happens, always remember and apply the quote from Gandhi: **'Whatever you do will be insignificant, but it's very important that you do it'.**

Part 3:
Selling Beliefs

'Live your beliefs and you can turn the world around.'

Henry David Thoreau

'Your mission becomes your constitution: the solid expression of your vision and values. It becomes the criterion by which you measure everything else in your life.'

Dr Stephen Covey

We all have beliefs (from our environment, upbringing and experience) and they are all unique. But, ultimately, our beliefs drive our actions. So, in order to start getting to grips with slow selling properly, we need to start by examining some 'traditional' selling beliefs, and put forward some 'slow selling' alternatives.

(We will then move on to 'Emotions', 'Actions' and 'Measures' in turn).

Making money

'Speedy Selling' Processes unwittingly come from the overriding belief that the 'Shareholder is King'. Many organisations state that the 'Customer is King', but the true test of belief is how Organisations act ... not what their marketing says!

In other words, most organisations' top purpose (by far) is to 'MAKE MONEY'... first and very much foremost. Only once they have done that, they then believe they can have the resources and time to focus on delivering a great customer experience.

As an Organisational Director, you may say: 'That's not true: we're very focused on our customer'. But consider the following:

- What do your front-line people really believe?
- What level of unquestioning true loyalty do you have from your customer?
- How much of your business comes TO you from reputation and referral vs. how much do you have to GO AND GET from 'traditional' sales processes?
- What figures do you target and motivate your people on: money figures or customer experience figures?
- What key figures determine 'success' from your shareholders' point of view: what measures and figures

do they judge you on, on a monthly, quarterly and annual basis?

In a nutshell: the 'traditional' business is run primarily to make money: shareholder value is what matters first, and the 'Mission' of the Organisation (if it was brutally honest) would be 'To make an ever-increasing profit at all costs'.

Here's a classic 'unbalanced Mission' that we have come across (from a double-glazing sales company!)

Our vision for growth offers unlimited financial rewards to those individuals who share in our success. We passionately believe in helping people realise their dreams by working with our Organisation.

The 'Slow Selling' countertype

What we are NOT saying is that Organisations shouldn't want to make a good profit. Indeed, the reverse is true: without good profits you can't survive or develop: we understand that! But what we ARE saying is that, (in the world of the empowered customer and two-way mass communication), you need to slow down! If you change the order and maintain a healthier balance between measures, you will find 'doing business' much easier and more profitable in the long term.

Natural principles of human behaviour are king: **Shareholders can only gain true long-term value after you have developed remarkable levels of customer loyalty and reputation.**

Your 'Mission' perhaps needs to change to something like:

- 'Customers and Principles come first: then the profits will follow, not the other way around'.
- 'We are not here to only 'make money', we are here to do what we do so well that people want to be associated with us and loyal to us'.
- 'Our true aim is to be 'remarkable' for all the right reasons!' (And then we'll also be profitable).

Explanation: your 'true beliefs' will guide all your strategy, process and behaviour like a compass. Unless you specifically state them in terms similar to what we've suggested above, your Organisation will default to the 'We're here to make a good profit' belief … and your strategy, processes and behaviour will be sub optimal from the customers' point of view. The reason that this is the case is basic biological fact: remember 'Fight or Flight': we're animals striving to survive and thrive on this planet, and our natural instinct is to consider our own needs first, often without consideration of the other person's need at all. It takes above average emotional intelligence to rise above this, get our beliefs in the right order and focus on generating great levels of customer experience, loyalty and reputation first … in the firm belief that then, and only then, will remarkable levels of sales and profits follow for the long term.

Slow Tip:
Slowly discover and distil your 'true purpose': a higher purpose than 'making money'. A purpose that energises your people and attracts customers like bees around a honey pot.
- We call this your 'customer focused mission'.

'Slow Selling' starts with your beliefs.

Case study:

- We worked with a new gastropub in Somerset. When we started working with them they'd just taken over a failing business taking under £1000/week.
- The business was refurbished and the whole ethos, strategy, processes, training and measures were trained and changed from 'We're here to get customers' to 'We're here to make sure everyone leaves with a smile on their face, keen to return'.
- This wasn't just introduced as a bland phrase, it was ingrained into
    - Job title
    - Terms and Conditions
    - Training
    - Weekly updates and development sessions
    - Measurement
    - Reward
- The result was that within 18 months turnover had increased by 1200% and the pub won a National Quality Award

Having a strong pitch

'Speedy Selling' Processes state the need to 'have a strong pitch' and 'sell the sizzle, not the sausage'. They teach systems and processes to 'pitch to the customer', and put in processes and systems to follow this up.

In reality this results in

- Marketing hype that often strays dangerously away from reality.
- Tag lines and clever words to interrupt the customer.
- Healthy customer cynicism and active avoidance of adverts and hype (after all, how many cosmetic products do you have to buy to be 'worth it'!?!)
- Bland unfulfilled promises of 'Exceptional Customer Service' and 'Leading Edge Innovation' from 'Best in Class' providers … !

All in all, a lot of activity, cost and aggro: often for very small results … a bit of a waste. But 'what's the alternative?' you may say … in a world of hyper communication you have to shout louder and be more noticeable in order to get noticed.

Well … yes … and no. Of course, if you give a really great deal and manage to get it on the front page of Google, you'll probably be inundated with potential customers. But how sustainable would this be over the long term? You'd have to work very hard to both keep the deal 'great' and keep yourself in the right place. This is a strong pitch, but adds unnecessary cost and complexity to your process. Maybe there could be an alternative … that makes life much easier for you and your customer, and allows you to make much more profit over the long term for a lot less aggro …

Here's a good example of 'having a great pitch': this is a sales instruction inside a company:
- Set the sales pitch scene by outlining how the sales pitch will be delivered and establish the need to change.

... a bit of an arrogant assumption?

The 'Slow Selling' countertype to 'Having a Strong Pitch' is:

All sales are, at source, driven by human relationships ... and **in human relationships slow is 'great' and fast is 'poor'.**

Slow Down! Focus on your customers' needs and how they are best met, whether they buy from you today or not: if you build trust and 'genuineness' into all you do, your brand will be at the top of the pile when someone wants to buy something in your market.

Of course, not EVERY customer will find you, maybe not even a majority will find you: many customers will be tempted elsewhere by strong pitches and flashy deals: but these are the customers who are fickle, and will get into bed with whoever looks sexiest at the time (in both appearance and price). These are not customers who will remain loyal (they were only loyal to the offer, not to the genuine article), and they are certainly NOT customers who will buy up, buy across, come back and recommend you to their friends. In short, you cannot build a long term sustainable profitable brand with these people ... you just can't.

> **Slow Tip:**
>
> Focus all marketing and sales 'pitch' on building trust and emotional value to the customer first: the 'irresistible pitch' can then follow without the customer laughing at you.

- For proof of this, just look at any brands and organisations that offered continual 'great deals' 10 years ago, and then see how many are still doing so, or even in business today.

Be honest about what your product is truly great for and what it is not: if the potential customer isn't right for you, the last thing you want to do is sell them something for the 'wrong' reasons: this will just destroy your reputation and massively inflate your costs of returns and after-sales. But also be really clear about what you're truly great at.

Focus on building trust and relationships before any 'irresistible pitch'.

Case study:

Richer Sounds

- Richer Sounds are highly successful HiFi and TV retailers in the UK. They don't have flashy stores in prime locations, nor do they continually promote their brand. What they do do is train their people to blow the customer's socks off at every step of the way, sell high quality goods, and make sure they're priced competitively (and offer a no nonsense guarantee on price). The result is that they have continued to enjoy huge levels of customer loyalty and reputation, and expand and be profitable in a market that's seen two larger competitors (and many other retailers) go bust.

Sales Processes and Techniques are Key

'Speedy sales processes', emphasise the importance of process and technique. They are extensively trained and many writers and consultants get very rich promoting more and more 'quick fix' process and technique answers to the problem of ineffective sales.

The problem is that almost all these systems are focused on 'push': i.e. the win/don't care attitude of 'getting a sale' by offers and attrition (never mind what the customer wants).

For example: a call from a local double-glazing Company the day before writing this:

- Start with permission: 'Is it OK to talk?'
    - 'Yes' (we want some material for the book)
- Small question: 'Do you own your house?'
    - 'Yes'
- Another question: 'Would you like to know how to add value to it in a way that pays for itself' (Strong Pitch!)
    - 'Yes, that'd be good'
- Statement of urgency: 'We have people in your area / limited time offer / etc'
    - 'Go on'
- Alternative close: 'What time of the day would suit you best for an appointment: am or pm'
    - 'Pm'
- Finish off: So, I'll make an appointment with Mr Bloggs for next Tuesday at 3pm: is that OK?'
    - 'Yes, but he'd be wasting his time.'
- (Now flummoxed: this shouldn't have happened / wasn't in the script). 'Sorry?'
    - 'He'd be wasting his time' (I'm being disingenuous as part of my research, I'm not normally this obtuse … honest!).
- 'I'm sorry, I don't understand'
    - 'Well, you haven't asked me the right question'

- 'I'm confused: what do you mean?'
  - 'Well, surely, if you're trying to sell something, it'd be a good idea to ask if I needed it or wanted it?'
- 'But I asked you if you wanted to increase the value of your home in a way that pays for itself'
  - 'Can I tell you what the right question is?'
- 'OK' (a bit unsure …!)
  - 'Are you able to fit double glazing in your home?'
- 'Are you able to fit double glazing in your home?'
  - 'No, we're listed and in a conservation area'
- 'OK, sorry, thanks for your time'
  - 'My pleasure' (Smug git).

The 'Slow Selling' countertype

Slow Down! It's win/win or no deal today: **No one cares how much you know until they know how much you care**. Your sales processes need to be more honest, less disingenuous and MUCH slower: this will get you results MUCH faster.

Get the right people with the right beliefs and abilities first, you can train them on systems and process 2nd.

Your systems and processes need to be win/win (or no deal today): NEVER anything else.

Let's re run the above scenario with 'Slow Selling Techniques'

- Start with permission: 'Is it OK to talk?'
  - 'Yes' (that's OK, they were polite)
- Small question: 'Do you own your house?'
  - 'Yes'
- Another question: 'I represent a home improvements Company, local to you, and wondered if you'd be OK if I asked you a few questions about your house and your situation, to see if we could perhaps help add value to you, or not, and either is ok. Can I take a moment to explain a little more, as I know I've phoned you out of the blue and you have no reason to trust anything I say?'

- 'Yes, that's fine'
- 'OK, well the name of my Company is [XYZ] and there are two things I need to explain to you in order for you to decide whether you want to carry on with this call or not. It genuinely won't take long'
  - 'Go on'
  - 'Thanks: now the two things I need to tell you about are ….

Pushy

'Speedy Selling' Processes focus on 'hooking the customer' and use 'pushy' sales techniques to get the customer interested and make a sale quickly. We see these all the time dressed up in

> ### Slow Tip:
>
> Slow your sales processes down: focus on adding real value (that means value to the customer, according to their 'tea' emotions, not yours) first.
>
> The other stuff can follow (when it's aligned!)

words like:

> 'Limited time special offer!'
>
> 'Hurry, must end soon!'
>
> 'It's double discount weekend!'

You see it all day every day in adverts, and in person it might look something like this:

Prospect: "I'm not sure if I'm ready to commit to this purchase yet. I'm going to need more time to think about it."

Salesperson: "I understand. But I should let you know that this reduced price that I'm offering you today is only available until the end of the week. Why don't I give you a couple days to think about it and touch base with you at the end of the week?"

The 'Slow Selling' countertype

Slow down and 'Be Pully' not 'Pushy': attract customers through quality and style, and then develop the relationship through personalisation, service, transparency and trust.

THE CUSTOMER'S REAL NEEDS

T — trust
E — easier better life
A — attention

In this type of selling, instead of trying to 'push', you **build relationships of trust, loyalty and desire** through behaviours of

Trustworthiness

Easier or better life

Attention

Case study:

Abel & Cole.
- Abel and Cole sell vegetable boxes and general groceries in the UK. They focus on Organic and high quality: this is a difficult and competitive market. The way they trade is on service and personality that builds massive customer loyalty, and gently persuading customers to recommend them to their friends with consistent quirky and up-front promotions.
- Loyalty is generated through:
  - Obsessive attention to quality
  - Well trained delivery people, focused on service and personalisation
  - Extra items added for free to 'spice up' the box (eg extra lemon to stuff a chicken).
  - Continual interest on the website with weekly focuses and offers that are generous but aimed at existing customers (not new ones)
  - Obsessively remarkable handling of any complaints or issues: the customer is always believed and they go out of their way to blow your socks off in problem situations.
- Referrals come through continual quirky and valuable requests: one we had recently stated: 'Things in threes are the Bees Knees', and asked us to:
  - Open this envelope
  - Write your account number on each voucher
  - Give the vouchers to your favourite people so they can try one of our organic fruit and veg boxes
- Not rocket science, but well thought through, attractive and fun!

www.abelandcole.co.uk

Marketing drives sales

'Speedy Selling' Processes are driven by marketing: and the marketing's aim is to drive more sales to the brand. This is driven by a belief that looks a bit like: In a world where most people's basic needs are met, we have to pander to their material wants and prostitute our principles in order to achieve sales goals. Nothing wrong with this to some extent, but the consumer rapidly gets to the state where they don't want more, and in fact more is becoming detrimental to them.

For example: mass market lager. The beer industry has for many decades promoted 'mass market lager' (because it's easy to produce and store consistently, and easy for the customer to like quickly). This has led to the creation of some very strong brands and some very clever and insistent marketing.

- It has also led to poor product quality levels, endemic alcohol problems and now massive consumer backlash!

Slow Tip:
- Change your marketing step by step: focus on how to get the most helpful message you can in front of the right audience.
- Never focus on how you can hype up your offer and make it look sexier than it really is: the truth will out!

The 'Slow Selling' countertype

Slow Down! Customer opinion drives sales.

The world has changed: the market is now transparent and **the customer can and will decide their own wants without the marketers pushing them**: they can and will also research about our product and service via reviews from other customers: they will seek differentiation, quality and style.

It is no longer a marketing driven world, it's a CX (customer experience) and CID (customer's individual desires) driven world. Taking it slowly and getting it right for the long term is the only effective marketing strategy in this new world.

> **Case study:**
>
> The rise of craft and cask beer.
> - A great example of this change can be seen in the beer market around the world with the rise of craft and specialist beers, often swiftly growing and outselling their heavily promoted rivals (and often with little or no promotion of their own). And as soon as customers realise that the world holds much more rewarding experiences outside of the heavily promoted mass market, they are extremely unlikely to revert to old habits!

Advertise

'Speedy Selling' Processes advocate: The more people see you, the more they'll buy. But, although there is still some truth to this (people like things they are 'familiar' with, whether they're any good or not), this is changing rapidly.

- With the rise of the Internet and social media, people now have a worldwide glut of choice (in both products and services), and research shows that customers trust other customers' reviews at least three times more than any advertising. [Source: https://www.marketingweek.com/2018/08/06/consumers-do-not-trust-traditional-advertising-channels/] And this is rising year on year as reviews become easier and more ubiquitous.

The 'Slow Selling' countertype

The 'Slow Selling' countertype recognises this change in the market: this reversion back to 'old fashioned' principles of reputation and genuine quality and instead advocates:

Take it slowly: The consumer is getting smarter every day: they can and will find out more about you through their own sources, than through any adverts you'll be able to produce. **Focus on quality and being genuinely 'remarkable' in what you do**: then make it easy for your

Slow Tip:

- Make a continual reduction in advertising spend a key success measure of your business, while also expecting continual sales improvement. This will force everyone out of their comfort zones for all the right reasons.

customers to spread your message: the sales will then start to take care of themselves.

Adverts mainly massage our own ego and have very little direct results. A full page in a glossy mag can cost $'000's, this may be worth the cost in order to spread the image you're looking for, but, in reality, customers are way more likely to buy according to your reputation and track record ... as spread by your previous customers.

Remember: 'genuinely remarkable' businesses rarely advertise: their customer queues are already too long.

Advertising can still work if consistent, focused and targeted: this does not mean the end of advertising, it just means the end of advertising as a means of creating false demand. Advertising now needs to be genuine, genuinely valuable, remarkable and consistent with what you actually deliver.

> **Case study:**
>
> - A quality Kitchen retailer in the UK was experiencing trouble with too high overheads (shops and marketing costs) compared to the sales this generated for them. We worked with them from the roots up, looked at what was 'genuinely remarkable' about them, rebuilt the business (and all it's attendant noises) around this, and by a process of serious focus and small steps managed to almost halve marketing overheads whilst boosting sales enquiries and conversions by over 25%.

First impressions

'Speedy Selling' Processes

First impressions must be amazing at all costs: we can then relax.

This is very similar to the hackneyed stories of second-hand car sales people: they're all over you before you 'sign on the line', but afterward you can't even get them to answer the phone.

The 'Slow Selling' countertype

> The true value of a customer does NOT lie in ONE sale!

Slow down! First impressions are very important, but **it's what you actually deliver / what you do after the sale or when you don't have to that determines your true long-term reputation and success**. The true value of a customer does NOT lie on ONE sale it lies in long term (maybe lifetime) loyalty and the costless acquisition of countless new customers (because the one customer actively spread the word about how remarkable you are).

Slow Tip:

Work on 'blow your socks off' 2nd, 3rd and 4th impressions before focusing on 1st impressions.

Case study:

- Insurance Companies seem to fall into two categories:
    - Those that 'get it' and
    - Those that don't
- Those that get it focus on service, speed, quality, transparency and genuine value (and so have high levels of customer loyalty and the best quality customers)
- Those that don't focus on price comparisons and 'special offers' to get new customers ... and then hike up the premium on renewal, counting on customer apathy to make them profits, (and so have low levels of customer loyalty and the lowest quality customers).

The customer is always right

'Speedy Selling' Processes

'The customer is always right'

Usually in B2B, where the buyer may have large repeat orders and will know as much as the seller, they can almost hold the seller to ransom (and this is a common complaint we pick from B2B sellers before we work with them).

Suppliers often reciprocate by putting in hidden costs and hidden price rises.

The result is a lose/lose game that benefits no one in the long term, produces sub optimal quality, broken contracts and lots of work for the lawyers!

Conversely, in a B2C situation, this glib phrase can cause frustration (customers aren't always right, they can be very difficult and annoying at times, and everyone knows it), which, in turn causes resentment and, through this, poor service … a lose/lose outcome that's far too common.

We've never forgotten, in our time in the leisure industry, there was a common saying: 'This would be a great business if it wasn't for the bloody customers!'

The 'Slow Selling' countertype

Natural principles of human behaviour are always right: **the customer is NOT always right … but they ARE always the customer!**

Slow Down! In long term relationships, it's genuinely 'win/win' or it should be no deal today.

If everyone is always having to check the trust of the other party, it's not much of a relationship (!) and lots of time will be wasted which could much more profitably be used to build our business.

The only way to have a proper B2B relationship is to build a

> **Slow Tip:**
>
> Teach and continually publicise the **'The customer is not always right … but they are always the customer'** slogan across your team.
>
> Start investigating win/win agreements as a powerful sales tool (further info later)

win/win relationship of mutual long-term trust and benefit, where we both genuinely help each other build their businesses.

B2C relationships should be carefully planned, using win/win systems, to ensure that the customer is properly educated, and treated remarkably throughout the process.
This takes courage, needs the ego to be 'left at the door' and high-quality training and tools to make this work. We can clearly see from the world around us how rare it is to see this working in practice.

We suggest using a simple, but powerful, system called 'win/win agreements': these are powerful not only for sales, but also for delegation, coaching, problem solving, leadership and management (which are of course just different types of 'sales' anyway!).

Case study:

Guy's first proper job was as a Beer Rep in the SE of the UK. He had good brands and prices (as did all his competitors) and he had a patch where there were 80+ active and profitable accounts and about 30 'good prospects', but the patch was in decline and competitors were taking away accounts.

- His start point was always to focus on service, promptness and reliability to his existing customers, but he also focused on 'slow selling' to the prospects.
- He did this by calling on them in a professional rotation, and only going in when he had something of value to offer them for nothing (usually trade information pertinent to their specific business). He never tried to sell his products and instead focused on building a reputation of trust and 'genuine remarkableness' through just 'trying to be genuinely helpful to them whether they bought a lot of product from him or not'.
- Of course, sooner or later their existing supplier would cock up a delivery, so who would they call first to try and help them solve their problem? The person who they genuinely trusted.
- Eventually, in 3 years, he had all but 6 as regular customers … with no 'special deals' or 'fast selling'. He didn't know it was called 'slow selling' at the time: it just seemed like common sense and manners!

The seller is in control (in B2C situations)

'Speedy Selling' Processes

In B2C situations the customer is often ignorant of the real situation: the seller knows the market, what the full picture is, what's really on offer, what's a good deal and what isn't.

Customers are often seduced by sexy marketing (often backed up by sales systems that are aimed at hoodwinking the customer).

> ### Slow Tip:
>
> Slow down: remember the customer really is now in control, and your market and reputation are truly transparent.
>
> Focus on REAL value and integrity: always do the best and fairest deal you can do: assume the customer knows as much about your market as you do, then blow their socks off!

A good example of this are carpet or furniture retailers that artificially inflate prices so they can offer 'half price deals' (that are actually the correct full price … for often substandard goods).

The 'Slow Selling' countertype

If you mislead the customer, they will never trust you and not only that, they'll make sure all their friends are similarly warned not to do business with you. And if you do it too often, or it becomes the 'norm' in your marketplace (as it seems to be in Insurance, Utilities, Furniture, Kitchens, Cars and Carpets), then you will teach the customer never to pay the full price; never to trust what you tell them; and never to be loyal to any brand, but instead always to shop around on price as first option.

Slow down, focus on REAL value, understate yourself and over deliver then you will grow steadily and sustainably through repeat business, reputation & referrals, no matter how much you COULD manipulate your customer if you chose to.

Case study:

- Market Carpets, Devon: in 50 years Market Carpets have grown from 1 small edge of town centre shop in a sleepy provincial town, to the No 1 carpet retailer in Devon. They have done this without 'limited time sales', without 'special offers' and without 'amazing cut price deals'. They trade solely on reputation, referrals and loyalty: and those of us who use them regularly wouldn't dream of going anywhere else. Indeed, when I asked them, over 50% of their customers never even ask what the price is, they are regular customers (builders, furnishers, carpet layers and property owners), and they just KNOW the price will be fair and competitive … and the service and ease of dealing with them will be GREAT! No fuss, very little marketing, and very rewarding for customers and the business.

The buyer is in control (in B2B situations)

'Speedy Selling' Processes

In B2B situations the customer is often in a strong negotiating position: they may be negotiating for large quantities over long terms, and the targets and perceived success' of the seller could be dependent on their actions. This can theoretically put the buyer 'in control'.

This can then result in all sorts of dysfunctional behaviours on both sides, with:

- Buyers being unreasonably 'tough' and requiring the seller to trade on terms that are unsustainable
- Sellers employing smoke and mirrors to hide charges, artificially inflate prices etc etc

A good example of this are Government contracts that so often end in poor results / overspends / or even supplier meltdown.

And the output of this immature and dysfunctional way of trading (apart from sky high levels of stress) is a pointless cat and mouse game, where everyone underperforms and the outputs are usually even worse: a classic 'lose/lose' scenario!

The 'Slow Selling' countertype

The answer to this conundrum lies in employing all the 'Slow Selling' systems and processes methodically with the customer.

- Put in place up front win/win agreements that are designed to get a genuine win/win (or 'no deal today') outcome. The customer has to win, because they have to have reliable, cost effective suppliers, and the supplier has to win because they need to be able to deliver consistent quality, continually invest in improvement and make a fair profit.

- As a 'seller' be sure to have the meeting and make this agreement up front: know where your REAL 'no deal today' point is (and don't forget your hidden costs and your need to continually develop and improve your systems and products).
- Always be helping, and adding value to actual and prospective customers (and the market), no matter what happens: ensure all prospective customers know that they can speak with you at any time, without being 'sold to'.
- Obsessively focus on building a reputation for quality, honesty, helpfulness and transparent value.
- Never fall for the 'loss leader deal … and then we'll buy lots more from you' offer, unless this is a key part of the written long-term win/win contract (and is done as a contribution to help them win and keep more customers, not just to make a quick and easy extra bit of profit to make the figures look right for the year end).

Of course it isn't easy: doing the right and effective thing never is!

Linear sales processes

'Speedy Selling' Processes advocate and teach a linear, step by step approach to take the customer along the route YOU want them to go down: you have all the energy, time and power, and you repeat this until either you wear them down and they buy … or they hate you so much they'd NEVER do business with you!

We know this sounds ridiculous, but just stop and think about it the next time you receive yet another flyer or email selling message: this is exactly what they're doing!

So why on earth would they do this? Because it's easy to do (especially in these days of 'smart' technology) and the marketing department have to prove they're doing something, so they generate lots of activity!

It often seems to us that the smarter the technology gets, the dumber the operators of that technology become!

The 'Slow Selling' countertype

Take it slowly: aim for loyalty, reputation and remarkability first … the sales will then follow.

> **Slow Tip:**
>
> Have circular sales systems.
>
> Build customer feedback in as the #1 continuous improvement and development driver: done properly, this won't let you down.

Remember that everyone is different: understand customer needs first: keep listening and understanding, using open questioning and helping systems.

Build customer trust slowly step by step.

Have circular systems and customer sales flow charts aimed at building value to the customer and giving them the opportunity to buy at any time: your customer will come to you from any direction: you're not in control of the 'process' and their journey certainly isn't 'linear' any more.

Gather feedback continually and effectively, from sales and non-sales (and lapsed customers), and develop your systems and processed based on what you hear.

Case study:
- Ritz Carlton: the Ritz Carlton chain aims for 98% customer loyalty (the 2% are the ones they don't want to come back as they negatively affect the experience for the other 98%).
- So, over the years, with this as their 'Customer Focused Mission', they have developed and perfected systems to blow the customer's socks off at every step: from enquiry, to reservation, to on site experience, to post experience relationship.
- And, in consequence, they consistently significantly outperform rivals in profitability and growth, not through acquisition or building new sites, but from loyalty and growth of the lifestyle brand.
- Here's a great extract from their leadership website

- We no longer live in a transactional economy. We live in a relationship economy, or as author Joseph Pine describes it, an "*Experience Economy*." This means we are developing relationships with customers and patients and meeting each person's unique needs. While there are a few businesses like Walmart that thrive simply based on low prices—most organizations will find greater profitability by offering outstanding service, building authentic relationships and cultivating customer loyalty. One of the best ways to convince decision-makers to join the relationship economy is to share data that supports a customer-centric approach. According to research by *Bain & Company*, it costs six- to seven-times more to acquire a new customer than retain an existing one, and yet, many organizations devote more of their efforts to acquisition rather than loyalty. At The Ritz-Carlton, we have found that our fully engaged guests—our most loyal customers—stay more room nights in a year and spend $25 more per day. When you see customers as transactions, you try to collect "nickels and dimes" from them, but when you see customers as relationships, your organization wisely spends "nickels and dimes" on the customers.

- www.ritzcarltonleadershipcenter.com

Hidden agendas

'Speedy Selling' Processes

- Never tell the customer the whole truth: use every trick and technique you can to manipulate and 'drive' extra sales today.
- Have hidden clauses in your agreements to protect you against all sorts of problems that may arise in the customer relationship.
- Manipulate the customer's decision by using leading body language and misleading language.
- Make sure your 'complaints processes' and guarantees are hard to find and use.
- If you offer a guarantee, make sure that it is very conditional and excludes all sorts of things and gives you lots of get out opportunities.
- Online manipulation of prices and links to mislead the customer.
- No more explanation needed on this one: we all see it far too often!

The 'Slow Selling' countertype

Take it slowly.

A sale for the wrong reason today is a relationship and reputation disaster tomorrow.

Be genuine in your desire to 'get it right' no matter what: have an open agenda that you share with the customer.

Have a brilliant problem resolution system aimed at not only resolving the problem, but also blowing the customer's socks off through it!

Slow Tip:

Ensure you have no 'hidden agendas': check that the customer is told everything up front that you'd like to know if you were the customer.

Proactively look for opportunities to offer simple, open, transparent guarantees, then promote them as much as you can: they may cost a little to do properly, but see this as a marketing investment in customer loyalty and reputation: it's worth it!

Promote no quibble guarantees: they not only give your customer confidence (and seriously increase sales per visit and sales conversion rates), but also keep you on your toes by ensuring you always perform to your highest standard.

(Note: we run a 'no quibble guarantee' on all our work, and we are often asked: 'Isn't that a bit dangerous?'. Our response to this is: 'Not at all. We'd want everyone to be delighted with the work we do, and, if not, we'd want them to tell us first, so we can fix it, rather than be underwhelmed and moan about us behind our backs'.) Just common sense really, put into simple, up front, proactive, clear statements.

Incidentally, research shows that, usually, over 90% of 'underwhelmed customers' never share this opinion with the business in question: they simply leave and don't come back (and often tell their friends not to bother as well). [Source: https://beyondphilosophy.com/15-statistics-that-should-change-the-business-world-but-havent/]. **This is a HUGE hidden cost to most businesses**: far better to take a (very small) cost up front, through a transparent guarantee, and then blow people's socks off by responding brilliantly to any calls on that guarantee.

Case study:

Lakeland Plastics: here's their guarantee:

- From everyday utensils and preserving basics, to never-seen-before cookware; if they've made it into our range, you can be sure they'll be long-lasting and offer great value for money. We are so confident of this that every item is backed by our guarantee, if you're not delighted with your purchase or our service, or find the same product elsewhere for less, please tell us so that we can put it right. It's this kind of dedication to service that has gained us such a loyal customer following over the years.

Case study:

Webuyanycar.com
- A recent advert featured a man speaking to the camera about how it was possible to save time when selling a vehicle through We Buy Any Car. The man stated "I'm going to say something radical in this advert for WeBuyAnyCar.com. I might have got more money for my car, if I'd sold it privately. Yeah I said it. But I asked myself, how much do I value my time? Am I gonna put up with all that hassle for a bit more money? Would you?" The final scene featured a voice-over which stated, "Value your time? Enter your reg number now at WeBuyAnyCar.com, the UK's favourite car buying service."

The sales and marketing funnel

'Speedy Selling' Processes teach that you should 'have a 'sales & marketing funnel' designed to take your customer down a route'. The idea is that your pour as many people into the top, via clever and hyped up marketing, then, if you get enough people in, and you keep pushing, some will fall out at the bottom and become customers! Hurrah!

SALES

THE SALES & MARKETING FUNNEL

Then you keep repeating this, with ever increasing velocity. (And never mind the 90%+ of potential customers who you upset and lose along the way).

The 'Slow Selling' countertype

Customers come from anywhere at any time for any reason. The Internet empowers them to find you much more easily than you can find them. Indeed, they can find out more about your products, performance, reputation and competition in an instant than you probably know yourself. The marketing input into the funnel is no longer your main long-term business builder.

Have circular systems that are designed to build relationships and loyalty at all stages and continually evolve and develop these through feedback … as an overriding business strategy … in the sure belief that, if you do this well, the sales will follow … not the other way around.

Slow Tip:

Keep developing and improving your circular systems.

Draw and train the 'Slow Selling System' ... not the funnel!

Case study:

Amazon.
- Amazon focus, above all, on driving repeat business and customer loyalty. They know that people will come to them from many different routes (and of course they invest in exposure to make sure people can find them), but they focus, obsessively on customer experience, trust, retention, repeat sales cross sales and, above all, loyalty, to fulfil their mission of being 'the world's most customer-centric organisation'.

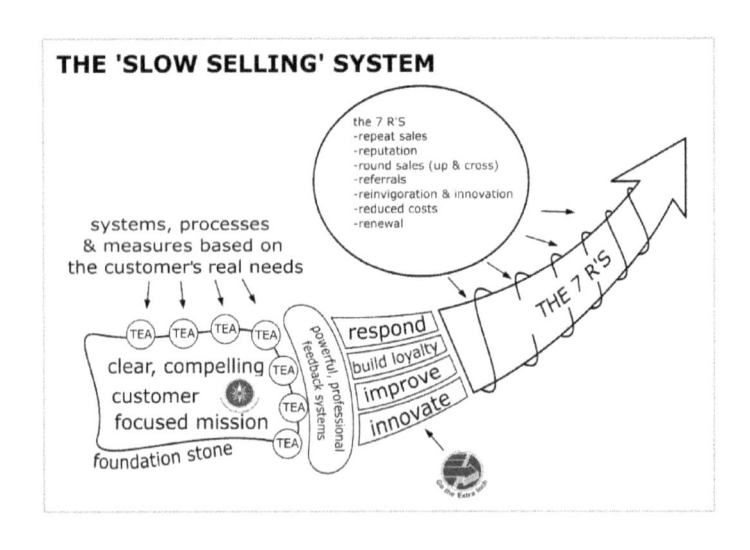

THE 'SLOW SELLING' SYSTEM

the 7 R'S
- repeat sales
- reputation
- round sales (up & cross)
- referrals
- reinvigoration & innovation
- reduced costs
- renewal

systems, processes & measures based on the customer's real needs

THE 7 R'S

respond
build loyalty
improve
innovate

powerful, professional feedback systems

clear, compelling customer focused mission

foundation stone

CRM systems

'Speedy Selling' Processes

Have a CRM system to drive more accuracy in your prospecting and follow up. Use the contacts in it to continually market your stuff to people and send out 'special offers'.

Example sales wording for a CRM system:

- By building an accurate, predictable and robust new customer pipeline you can make smarter decisions easily and quickly, and drive your business forwards. In order to drive this growth, you and your employees need to harness data-driven selling in order to minimise time lost to weak prospects and maximise value from new sales wins.

The 'Slow Selling' countertype

Use a CRM system for genuine CRM. Remember that the 'R' stands for 'relationship' ... not 'sale'.

Customers are not going to align with your 'system': use the system to genuinely build the relationship and over deliver on customers' needs by being proactively attentive to their subjective needs, making life easier and more streamlined for them, and taking ownership of the relationship.

Slow Tip:

Use your CRM system for CRM only ... then, and only then can you develop cross sales, up sales and referrals

Have circular systems that are designed to build relationships and loyalty at all stages and continually use the CRM system to evolve and develop these.

Have a wonderful feedback system built into your processes at every level, and integrate this with your CRM System so that you can not only blow your customers socks off consistently and continually, but also use this to drive improvement and innovation step by step, week by week, month by month … with the CRM system being your main tool for this.

> **Case study:**
>
> Carphone Warehouse:
>
> - I have been a long-term customer of Carphone Warehouse in the UK, I am constantly impressed and delighted by the way they use their CRM systems to interact with me consistently and brilliantly in our relationship. Whenever I deal with them, I feel confident and trusting that they will treat me excellently. A good example of this was when I visited a couple of years ago to buy a replacement charger: they reviewed my phone contracts while I was in the shop, suggested that they could save me money by changing some of the details (even though I was contractually committed to the current deal for another 8 or 9 months), and did exactly that on the spot! Now this is a way to build customer loyalty by using a CRM system for its true purpose. (Guy Arnold)

After sales follow up

'Speedy Selling' Processes

Put the customer into an automated selling system that sends them a continual sales messages whether they like it or not.

Use simplistic feedback systems that generate simple scores via web or e-mail based systems (because this is a quick, cheap and simple to do). Don't worry if that feedback you get isn't particularly high value, and isn't a reasonable percent of your customers: it's only PR anyway… Spend your real marketing money and give your real attention to your 'Sales and Marketing Systems' to try and drive more speedy sales by finding new customers.

Use simplistic loyalty schemes. We have to offer them because all our competitors do, so let's just replicate what everyone else does so we won't get left behind. Okay it costs us a bit of money, and we don't see any real value from it, but we feel we have to do it because everyone else is.

Mimimise spend in this area as it's a 'cost'. It's very simple really: spend on sales and marketing to get new customers is an investment, and spends on after sales is a cost, any fool knows this… Just ask an accountant!

The 'Slow Selling' countertype

Natural principles of human behaviour are king.

People judge you on how you treat them when there's nothing immediately in it for you.

Gather feedback obsessively and professionally after every sale and every 'no sales today thanks'.

Do this by having a remarkable system in place that adds value to the relationship, and don't forget to ask permission first in the right way too!

Be prepared to invest properly in after-sales with the unshakeable belief that it's 'the world's most effective marketing investment' in today's customer-empowered world.

Use reputation and referral systems to replace the simplistic 'loyalty scheme'. We will discuss these in more detail later, but, in a nutshell, these are systems that are designed to build strong and remarkable relationships of loyalty with your customers as an end in itself, so they naturally will want to come back to you as the first-choice next time, know what else they can buy from you, and recommend you enthusiastically to their friends and colleagues. All you need to do is to never forget these are your overriding aims, and start obsessively building remarkable systems and processes to make it easy for the customers to continue to engage with you and recommend you.

Change the name of your 'after sales processes' to 'long term relationship development processes.' The name you give something makes a HUGE difference. 'After sales' is an afterthought … 'relationship development' on the other hand is a key business strategy worth seriously investing in.

Slow Tip:

Change the name of your 'after sales' processes and/or department to 'future sales' or 'loyalty and reputation'.

Develop all processes to fit this new direction.

Please note: the order here is very important: you must get it right and be 'remarkable' BEFORE you ask for referrals and follow-up sales. Do it this way and your customers will be delighted to help you. But, if you ask for referrals BEFORE being genuinely remarkable, they will hate you for it.

Case study:

Plusnet;

- Plusnet are a UK based telephone company that pride themselves on customer service while also remaining competitive on price. As a customer of theirs, they don't always get it right, but they do have very customer focused systems, I would happily recommend them to friends, and I would be unwilling to use one of their competitors unless I had a strong recommendation from two or three people that I would trust.
- They have a very simple referral system which can be seen by following the link below. In a nutshell, they get it right by
    - Focusing on delivering remarkable service to existing customers above all else (so customers want to be loyal to them and consider what other products they can buy from them)
    - Then making it easy (above all else) for customers to refer them, and offering simple, valuable rewards to customers for doing so… With no upper limit!
    - https://www.plus.net/home-broadband/referrals/

After sales e-selling

'Speedy Selling' Processes

Bombard people (whether they are customers or not) who are on your 'system' with continual 'offers' and 'news'. (We received a classic one this morning: 'Be one of the first people in your area to see our new ad': How desperate do they think we are??).

Spend lots of money making the offers look bright and sexy. Focus on trying to persuade everyone on your e-mail list to buy more stuff through clever offers and seductive marketing.

The 'Slow Selling' countertype

Slow Tip:

Develop loyalty sales, cross sales, up sales and repeat sales effectively by developing relationships and getting your customers genuinely emotionally committed to you.

This can be hard and slow work: that's why so few organisations do it properly: that's also why you'll stand out from the crowd when you do it!

Slow Down! Treat existing customers better than new ones. Don't bombarded them with offers, treat them as genuinely special people who have trusted you enough to buy from you and **who should only ever be contacted with information or genuine offers that you would want to receive if you were them**, knowing what you know as the expert in your business.

Have genuine 'VIP clubs'. These should be clubs that offer special access to events and deals that cannot be accessed ordinary members of the public. You can also use these to build referrals by allowing the members of your VIP club to offer each deal to one (and only one) of their contacts. (But do not under any circumstances allow them to offer them to everyone and anyone: otherwise they lose their exclusive value).

Build relationships through professional feedback: Your feedback system must be

- ✓ Well thought through,
- ✓ Designed to add value to the customer in its execution,
- ✓ Enjoyable and motivating to the customer,
- ✓ Focused on what is important to the customer and what the customer wants to tell you (rather than what you want to ask the customer or what is important to you).

Doing it this way will add value to the customer and will help you understand them and give you all the information you need to build long term relationships with them. On top of this you need to respond to all feedback in two ways:

Direct response: you need to be able to respond to every piece of feedback directly and individually in an appropriate way.

Indirect response: you need to use the feedback to evolve and innovate and then you need to communicate this with your customers so they know that you have paid attention to what they told you.

Personalise the relationship to the customer's needs from feedback. Once you have this feedback you can then build it into your CRM systems to personalise the relationship and only engage with the customer according to the methods and content chosen by them.

Guarantee that the existing customer will always be treated as well as or better than any 'new customer offer', and that you'll be transparent with them. Add this to your guarantees: (then make sure you have adequate systems to deliver on this vitally important guarantee!).

> **Case study:**
>
> The Richer Sounds feedback system and VIP Club.
> - Richer Sounds are a UK based hi-fi and television retailer. They have legendary levels of team and customer loyalty. They also hold the Guinness world record for retail sales volume per square foot of retail space in their London Bridge store. Not coincidentally they have an obsessive customer feedback system and a wonderful high value VIP club. If I ever want inspiration, I call in to my local store to watch and listen! For more details please follow this link: https://www.richersounds.com/vip-club/

Direct and Indirect Response Systems

We mentioned above the difference between 'direct and 'indirect' response systems, and it's very important to understand why BOTH are vitally important to growing customer loyalty, reputation, referrals and, above all, long term sales.

Direct response systems are the systems you put in place to directly respond to the specific feedback, one by one, that you receive. **Indirect response systems** are the systems you put in place to make sure that all feedback is noticed, faced up to and proactively used to increase efficiency, systems, empowerment, motivation, loyalty, reputation and innovation … in general.

Some guidance on both:

Direct Response systems: we suggest you divide your response into three categories, using the ideas set out in the 'Net Promoter Score' system (for more information on this excellent system, please see www.netpromoter.com). These ideas suggest that your customers are either 'promoters' (they think you're remarkable and want to be loyal to you and promote you), 'passives' (they're 'satisfied' but not loyal or actively promoting you), or 'detractors' (they actively dislike dealing with you, switch suppliers as soon as they can, and will spread a negative reputation about you). We suggest you tailor your direct responses according to which camp they fall into:

- For 'promoters', you'd want to thank them for the feedback, then aim to engage with them and offer them VIP clubs and opportunities to benefit from loyalty and recommending you.

- For 'passives', you'd want to thank them for the feedback, then aim to engage with them to build the relationship until they become 'promoters'.
- For 'detractors', you'd want to thank them for the feedback, apologise for the problems they've spelt out to you, then ask permission to solve their problem. Then you deal with the problem using your remarkable 'problem recovery systems' in the same way as you would do if you'd received a complaint. (Note: we don't have space here to spell out what we mean by 'remarkable problem recovery systems', so if you'd like some help or guidance in this area, please contact us via www.slow-selling.com for free resources and advice in this area. Suffice it to say, that excellent work in this area can produce huge levels of customer happiness and loyalty ... sometimes significantly better than if they had been 'promoters' in the first place! This is a huge opportunity.)

Indirect response systems, are the continual improvement systems you put in place to ensure you continually learn and grow from all feedback, hone your systems, benefit from mistakes, empower your people better, drive continual innovation, reduce risk, and generally supercharge the motivation, loyalty and reputation of your external and internal customers.

- These systems are of course bespoke to any organisation, team or individual's specific circumstances, but they follow consistent and specific rules. If you'd like some help or guidance in this area, please contact us via www.slow-selling.com for free resources and advice in this area.

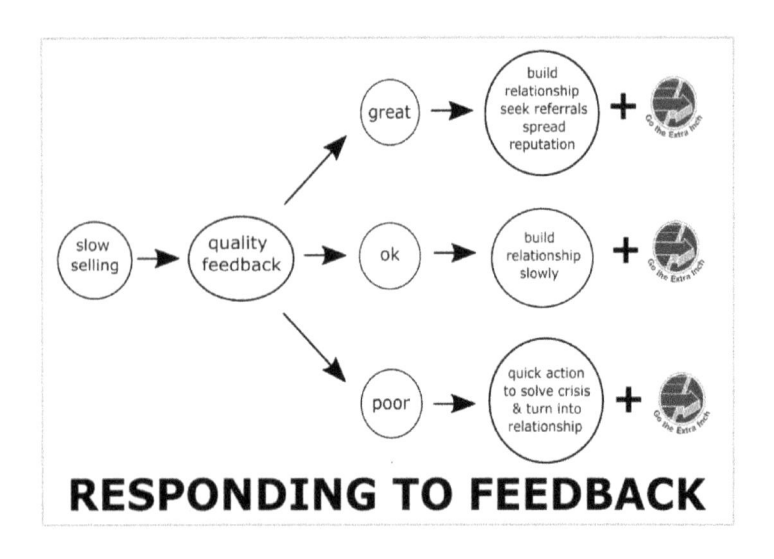

slow selling → quality feedback →
- great → build relationship, seek referrals, spread reputation + Go the Extra Inch
- ok → build relationship slowly + Go the Extra Inch
- poor → quick action to solve crisis & turn into relationship + Go the Extra Inch

RESPONDING TO FEEDBACK

Testimonials

'Speedy Selling' Processes

Use customer 'testimonials' to show what great people you are (even if they may be old/made up/paid for/only part of the story). Testimonials' make you look great because they are gushing and full of praise.

The 'Slow Selling' countertype

Testimonials aren't transparent and completely honest: they're filtered and selected.

Instead promote and gather transparent feedback, good and bad as a key business strategy: this demonstrates openness, trustworthiness and confidence (which are all VERY attractive traits to customers).

There's no such thing as bad feedback. Respond to feedback in such a way as to show how genuine you are and that you have nothing to hide (and you're not perfect). How you respond to feedback, good and bad shows the world what you're REALLY like.

Publish all feedback and responses transparently online (which builds more openness, trustworthiness and confidence): you are not perfect and neither is anyone else, but by doing this you clearly demonstrate a remarkable intent to wow the customer and prove that you are not frightened of putting your money where your mouth is. On top of this, you show that when you get it wrong you want to hear about it and are transparent and proactive about resolving any issues that any customers may have.

All of the above also helps you and your people stay sharp and on top of your game, in the same way that guarantees do … perhaps even more powerfully.

Slow Tip:
- Forget 'testimonials'
- Be courageous enough to proactively gather and publish all feedback transparently.
- Respond to all feedback effectively, and use it to learn, grow and build loyalty and reputation, both directly and indirectly.

Case study:

An online specialist Insurance seller

- We worked with an online specialist insurance seller who was struggling to make a name for themselves and to generate enough interest in their Brands without resorting to the online comparison websites (which don't really benefit the customer and, instead, leach profit that could instead be used to improve customer value). We advised them to not only proactively gather and publish feedback from all their clients, but also to publish a new website (and Facebook page) focused on 'travel insurance reviews' (i.e. a place where anyone buying this specialised travel insurance could openly publish reviews ... which our client could then respond to ... again openly!). The net result of this was a more than doubling of online enquiries in a year and a significant uplift in conversion rate for a very modest investment of time and money.

Doing Feedback in the right way

Many 'standard' feedback systems suffer from poor response rates and incomplete information gathered. In order to avoid this, it's essential to do your feedback in the 'right way'. To be successful at this, there are three key things to consider:

1. Right method for your market: you need to ensure the feedback method is appropriate for the relationship you have with your customer:
    a. For a 'transactional' relationship, a simple online system, done properly, works best
    b. For an 'emotional' relationship (e.g. a more complicated purchase, or a leisure purchase), a very carefully designed simple system that engages and adds value needs to be crafted: the key here is to get the process (demonstrates 'attention'), method (easy to use), attentiveness (so it's seen as genuinely of the highest importance at all levels) and response (so you build trust and loyalty). This is NOT simple to get right!
    c. For a 'partnership' relationship (e.g. most B2B or membership relationships), it needs to have all the qualities of the 'emotional' feedback system, AND be personal and in depth.
2. Holistic set up: this needs to be so much more than an 'add on' after a sale. We're suggesting that this needs to be a key, holistic, all-encompassing way of doing business, where the feedback is the powerhouse that drives all other actions, in the key belief (as above) that 'we're not here to sell our stuff, we're here to do something so remarkable that people will queue up to buy it' … and the key driver and compass of this approach is our remarkable feedback systems.

3. Permission based: doing feedback remarkably is as rare as hen's teeth. So customers are often bored, disengaged and unwilling to comply with your feedback requirements and systems. In order to address this effectively, you need to make sure your systems comply with the 2 rules set out above, and are also 'permission based'. What we mean by this is that you always ask permission to ask for feedback, before you ask it ... preferably at the start of the relationship. You may have an up-front statement like: 'We aim to be a supplier you love dealing with. In order to do this properly, we need to ensure we listen to you, properly, at all times. Please don't hesitate to ask us any questions or feedback to us at any time, and, when we've done our work, we'd like your permission to contact you to find out your opinion on our work and make sure we've done what we agreed and you're 101% happy with us'.

We don't have space here to spell out the full details of these suggestions, so if you'd like some help or guidance in this area, please contact us via www.slow-selling.com for free resources and advice in this area.

Part 4:
Selling Emotions

'Your intellect may be confused, but your emotions will never lie to you.'

Roger Ebert

'Feelings and emotions are the universal language and are to be honoured. They are the authentic expression of who you are at your deepest place.'

In this chapter, we explore the 'speedy selling' ideas on 'customer emotions' and suggest some 'slow selling countertypes' for your consideration …

Uncover needs

'Speedy Selling' Processes

You need to uncover needs of 'pain' or 'gain' in order to use these to sell more today.

Pain is much more preferable than gain, as people are far more motivated to move 'away' from pain than toward gain, so we need to focus all our marketing on creating perceived pain, and over exaggerating any threat in our marketplace. For example, the threat of looking bad if you don't use our cosmetics, of having dirty clothes if you don't use our (new improved formula!) chemical washing products, of being vulnerable to germs, prosecution, uninsured drivers etc

If we can't do this, we need to focus on special limited time offers!

And if we can't do this, we may need to think about 'bending the truth' a little to exaggerate the benefit of what we offer (a great and consistently annoying example of this would be a wholesaler valuing any free product they offer at the recommended retail price ...).

Here's a good example of a speedy sales process in action:

- 'Use the customer priority survey form to gain customer involvement and trust, and to identify any areas of concern they may have with their current XYZ product: an area of concern is termed a 'hotspot'.'

The 'Slow Selling' countertype

Slow down and build relationships of trust where the customer will then naturally turn to you and ask you how you can help them solve their problems again and again.

Build in guarantees into all you do. Educate the customer to make smart long-term decisions, add value through careful buying and the economics of scale. Work out what you can be the best in your limited market at, then REALLY nail it using the 4 BEAR principles.

Gather feedback to discover unfulfilled needs, then build in extra services or win/win partnerships with likeminded suppliers to fulfil them. This means you'll grow three dimensionally and sustainably.

Case study:

- We work with a professional feedback gathering service called 'Investors in Feedback'. This feedback finds out time and time again why people chose the client, what they love about them, why they'll stick with them and what else they can do to sell more to them. Then all the client needs to do is build all this feedback into their systems, SLOWLY, step by step, inch by inch.

- Then, and only then will they, genuinely, uncover the customer's REAL needs and systemise the consistent and continually improving delivery on, and over, these needs, so they consistently blow the customer's socks off and generate amazing long term sales.

- Some examples include:
    - Car hirers who also want accommodation (as well as a seamless experience)
    - Insurance buyers who also want VIP airport lounge access (as well as a trusted product)
    - Hotel Guests who want transport (as well as feeling cared for like a family member)
    - Osteopathic patients who want dietary help (as well as loving care)
    - Pub Owners who want staff training (as well as reliable products that customers want to buy)

And the list is endless!

Slow Tip:

- Look at all your processes and aim to stick to the principle of genuinely uncovering your customer's real needs in all you do.
- 'If we build relationships first, the results will then follow'.

Sell benefits

'Speedy Selling' Processes

Keep calm, listen, indicate approval, sell benefits: this is what we were taught as sales reps. Don't panic, don't ask them what they want (you might not have it and then you'll want to panic) … instead, use the above techniques to calm them and handle their objections, so you can then get back on track with selling to them.

When they've 'signed on the line', get out of there fast before you ruin it.

The 'Slow Selling' countertype

Natural principles of human behaviour are king: remember you're looking for a win/win long term relationship of mutual trust and mutual benefit: whether you get a sale today is of limited and secondary importance.

Keep calm, you've got nothing to be scared of, genuinely listen and build relationships: use the 'win / win agreement' (outlined in Appendix 2) to add genuine value. Tell them up front that your intent is to help them make the right decision whether they buy from you or not: (your reputation is worth more than a 'one off sale'), and give them confidence to open up. Have an upfront agreement that they'll make some sort of decision in this process. 'Peel the onion' with open questions, take great notes (consider using mind maps to give you control and to empower you to ask incisive and valuable questions). Read their body language and the tone and inflection in their voice to gauge (and put on the table) their REAL feelings and hopes. Pass on helpful information freely and outline the REAL options available to your client.

When they've talked (and you've peeled), then take time to reflect what they've said, including the emotions they've shared. Then (and only then) work together for 'win/win/ or no deal today' outcome.

Sell a relationship of trust, attention and ease of dealing with us as the prime objective ... the sales will follow later.

Slow Tip:

Sell a relationship of trust, ease and attention first: the physical sales will then follow.

Use win/win agreements to make this happen in reality.

Case study:

Timothy Taylor

Timothy Taylor are a small regional brewer in Yorkshire, England. They aim to brew to the highest possible standards, taking no shortcuts. This makes their beer more expensive to their customers (pubs and restaurants) than rivals' products.

Rather than compete on price, they concentrate on helping these customers maximise their retail trade, improve standards, match beer to food, and sell the Taylor products at a premium. Thus the pub gets an enhanced service, the pub's customer gets a better experience and more choice, and, by the way, they sell a lot of beer!

Their Sales Director, Paul Matthews says:

- We never compromise on our quality, and we never compromise on how we sell: We have a very structured price list and we never do deals or special offers on our iconic Landlord brand. We are very clear on what objections a customer would have to stock in our beer. They are:
  1. It's too expensive
  2. When it's on the bar it sells too well and stops us selling the other products
  3. It's difficult to keep
- So we look at all these customer concerns and decide how best to sell a product bearing in mind these very real feelings.

- The quality of the ingredients and finished product is why it sells so well when it is on the bar and therefore when we sell to people we try to understand their business and how our brand can deliver for them.
- And in this way our customers can see that our products add value to their whole business by delivering superior cash margin
- 9 out of 10 customers like this approach

Product Features

'Speedy Selling' Processes

The product's features and benefits must be heavily emphasised and polished up as much as possible.

The alloy wheels, the free estimates the touch screen system, the fast delivery, the impressive finish. The BIG DEAL!

Guy writes: 'An advert came through the door today for a 'die cast replica Ferguson T20 tractor': it has 'authentic details' and 'replicates hand finished touches' as well as having 'a certificate of authenticity': and all this for just £1.99 with 'free' postage and packing: I almost bought one, the offer was so good. But what do they REALLY want from me?'

The 'Slow Selling' countertype

Slow Tip:

Behave like a benevolent, knowledgeable adviser at all times.

Ask open questions to 'peel the onion' and find the customer's REAL needs.

Find solutions to the customers REAL needs, using features.

Take it slowly, get it right for the long term.

The customer can already find out about your features and those of your competitors at the drop of a hat, and, more importantly, they already know how these relate to their needs much better than you do. Be real, do your listening and peeling first (see above), then explain information that is factual and helpful to what THEY want (not what YOU want to sell), and explain how this relates to other options available to them.

You need to see yourself as a benevolent knowledgeable adviser to the customer who has no hidden agenda and no desire to get anything out of the encounter beyond unquestioned trust and goodwill … and then the sales will follow.

Case study:

- We worked with a Family run bespoke kitchen company. They were having trouble convincing potential customers to pay extra for their superior product, so were wasting a LOT of time on wasted quotes and follow ups.
- We implemented the systems outlined above, and helped them produce a simple booklet called 'How to get the best Kitchen for your needs, whether you buy it from us or not'.
- We changed the focus of the sales process exactly as outlined above.
- And the net result was that the pressure came off the customer, the designers could speak freely as if they were dealing with their best friend … and queries increased by 30%, while the sales conversion rate almost doubled. We wouldn't have believed it if we hadn't seen it for ourselves!

Find Solutions

'Speedy Selling' Processes

The customer wants a solution to their problem, so we need to talk all about solutions as much as possible.

So we need to make sure that we put the word 'solutions' in our name and use the word whenever possible.

The 'Slow Selling' countertype

Take it slowly, get it right for the long term.

Move off the solution: **it is not a solution unless it solves the customer's needs** (and by you calling it a solution, you are coming across as a bit arrogant and assumptive!). You CANNOT know what might be a good solution UNTIL you've listened and found out the REAL issues … and how the customer feels emotionally about those issues.

Use the slow selling principles and processes to work with the customer to understand the in-depth issues, wants and needs that they have, and together to work towards a genuine solution or to agree 'no deal today'.

In a nutshell you'd aim to do 6 things:

1. Remember your purpose: to help the customer first.
2. Tell the customer that you need to listen to them more to do this: then listen more
3. Ask soft open and peeling questions (Use the 'win/win agreement').
4. Make sure the conversation focuses on their problems and desired results.
5. Reflect these back until the customer genuinely believes that you've moved off the solution and are focused on their needs and issues.

Slow Tip:

Move off the solution: it isn't a solution unless is completely fulfils the customer's emotional needs.

Keep peeling the onion with open questions as much as you can.

6. Keep off the solution until they invite you to start working with them to find a solution … they are the judge of whether something is a 'solution' or not … not you!

Then, and only then can you genuinely talk about 'solutions'!

(Note: It IS OK to call yourself a 'solution finder' in your title or name, but we would suggest ONLY if you commit to the Slow Selling Principles and Processes in the first place).

Case study:

- A Professional Services outsourcing Company was disappointed in their sales conversion rate, and was relying on low priced introductory deals to win clients. We worked with them to 'move off the solution' and instead use the Slow Selling Principles and Processes to find the customers' REAL needs, and their emotional issues behind those needs, and thus tailor the proposed service they offered to fulfil those needs (and the emotional needs above all else). This resulted in a sales conversion rate improvement of almost 40% (and the removal of the need for 'special introductory offers').

Overcoming objections

'Speedy Selling' Processes

- Keep calm, listen, indicate approval, sell benefits.
- Have pre-thought through responses to objections: sell on uncertainty and fear of other suppliers and systems.

Slow Tip:

Slow Down!

Outline the Intent at the start of all meetings or proposals: you're there to help them make the best decision for them, whether they buy from you today or not

Change the word 'objection' to 'question'

Work through their questions genuinely and slowly, peeling the onion for their REAL needs.

The 'Slow Selling' countertype

'Objections' are normal human concerns and arise from one of the following issues:

- Lack of trust
- Lack of information
- Lack of budget
- Lack of confidence in your ability
- Belief that they can get the same product elsewhere better/cheaper

Take it slowly, set out your intent clearly: win/win or no deal today: you're there to help them make the best decision for them, whether it involves buying from you or not: and mean it genuinely (or don't do it ... the biggest 'objection' a customer will have is lack of trust through unaligned behaviour and body language)!

Work through their concerns genuinely using open questions and peeling the onion as above.

Build relationships of trust ... the sales will follow.

Case study:

- We were recently looking to buy a second-hand car. We visited three dealers, not knowing what we really wanted.
- In two of the dealers, they were keen to demonstrate all the features of the cars and had quick answers to any questions (usually 'objections' in their language) that we had. In both cases we weren't wowed and left unconvinced with an agreement to 'think about it'.
- In the third dealership, the sales rep sat us down and started by asking a full list of questions (with our permission) relating to our needs and desires (and possible 'objections'). We covered essential items such as fuel economy, running costs, space flexibility and 'real' cost to us (she asked questions about our personal work and finance situation so she could structure any offer in the most advantageous way to us, from payments and tax benefit point of view). Once we'd agreed all these points, buying the car was easy and pleasurable! A true win/win.

I am always reminded in this area of a wonderful sales rep from a catering services Company who successfully sold me a glass washer as a sex aid (because it would get me and my wife in bed an hour earlier every night)! With this sort of information, my 'objections' to price or performance criteria seemed insignificant! *(Guy Arnold)*

Tell / lead the customer

'Speedy Selling' Processes

Lead the customer down 'sales routes' using 'sales techniques'

The 'Slow Selling' countertype

Slowly develop systems to understand and help the customer make the best decision for them, no matter what. Only ever use any 'sales tools' if they add value to the process and the customer. Never take any actions or use any tools with any kind of hidden agenda.

Slow Tip:

Develop your sales systems slowly, using win/win mindset, listening and tools.

Case study:

- B2C: Amazon. Amazon give you a multitude of 'buying options' when you outline what product you want. We may see this a 'normal' now, but when it was introduced, it was revolutionary: all their competitors only offered products they could supply directly. It took guts and huge levels of emotional enlightenment to do this … and we all know the results.
- B2B: We worked with a wholesaler in highly competitive and price driven drinks market. We helped them to focus all their 'marketing' spend on supporting their customers and helping them develop their own business and generate more profits. They now don't need to advertise, their customers are 100% loyal, and they grow steadily every year through reputation and referrals.

Don't tell them unless they ask

'Speedy Selling' Processes

We never tell existing loyal customers about special deals coming up / more effective ways of buying / discounts if you buy in certain ways, because these are offers to lure new customers to us (like moths to a flame), and we can't tell our existing customers about them because that would reduce our profitability unnecessarily. Why would we want to give 'special offers' to customers we've already 'got'?

Slow Tip:

Be completely transparent in all your dealings and offers.

Offer no quibble guarantees.

Don't try to please everyone: identify your key customers and develop offers and processes that make you irresistible to them for all the right reasons.

Ignore the switching bargain hunters: recommend your competitors to them.

The only time we'd proactively tell a customer about them is when it would increase the size of their order today (e.g. volume discount), or if they threaten to leave us.

We never proactively tell a customer when their contract changes (they should remember the small print they signed 18 months ago!), we just charge them the extra and hope they don't notice. If they do notice, we apologise and put them on a new contract, but we pocket the extra cash we made from them in the meantime!

For example: many Insurance and Utility Companies who only offer 'special deals' on price comparison sites, but significantly increase prices on renewals (or when the customer goes out of contract). This drives customer disloyalty and is a MASSIVE unnecessary cost of customer switching.

The 'Slow Selling' countertype

Take it slowly: Long term reputation of trust and customer value is worth many times more than any short term saving in margin

Offer a 'Best rate guarantee' that means:

- ✓ We always tell the customer the best rate / best way to buy without them having to spend hours finding out.
- ✓ If there's a special offer being promoted, our existing loyal customers get access to it first.
- ✓ If there's a renewal we automatically offer the best rate.
- ✓ If there's a change that could benefit customers who are already tied in on contract, we offer it to them anyway (or, at worst, we tell them about it and guarantee to offer it to them when their contract comes up for renewal).

That way we build long term trust, loyalty, reputation and high levels of referrals.

Case study:
- Octopus Energy: a new UK energy Company who offer a 'best rate guarantee' (and really simple and customer focused communication), so the customer can relax and not worry about the bill.

Here's a quote from their website:

- It's a sad indictment of the energy industry's history that all energy suppliers have to put a statement on their website to say how they treat customers fairly.
- We started this business to do what is right for our customers, and right for the planet. We aim to be transparent and fair in everything we do not because we have to be - but because we want to be. Quite simply, It's what we're here for.
- That's why we fully support the [standards of conduct](#) from Ofgem.
- If you think we fall short of them, please let us know. If you find our actions anything other than fair, transparent, honest or appropriate - drop us an email to ThatsNotFair@octopus.energy and let us know.

Special introductory offers

'Speedy Selling' Processes

- Special offers and deals to get new customers.
- Not available to existing customers.

For example: many Insurance Companies / Cable TV / Phone Companies / Utility Companies etc

The 'Slow Selling' countertype

Employ the Slow Selling Principles and Processes outlined above, value customer loyalty above all else: this will drive reputation and referrals.

Be remarkable as standard, and then make referrals easy.

Have great 'thankyous' for referrals (not incentives: you want the customer to WANT to refer you (then you can thank them), not to be BRIBED to refer you).

Slow Tip:

Make sure all your systems and behaviours treat repeat customers better than new customers.

Don't get dragged into the race for the bottom with special offers.

Have VIP clubs with '1 referral only' deals only open to the club, as outlined above.

Case study:

We worked with a quality small Hotel chain who were struggling to let rooms and obtain reasonable rates in the 'shoulder months'. Using a powerful and proactive feedback system, we developed a VIP club, step by step over 18 months (and it's still developing and growing). The VIP club members have the following benefits:
- Priority booking in the high season and for special events.
- Discounted stays in shoulder months (on the best available price).
- Complimentary upgrades (varies each month).
- Preferential treatment prices in the Spa.
- Genuine partner benefits with quality local organisations.
- And the ability to offer this deal to ONE (and only ONE) friend every quarter.
- And, by the way, the chain also offers a 'best rate guarantee' which they control closely!

The result of adopting this strategy has been:
- Quicker filling of rooms at busy times (with regular guests and their friends)
- Significantly better occupancy rates in shoulder months with room rates increased by over 10%

Complicated pricing

'Speedy Selling' Processes

Make pricing complicated to maximise profits (eg Supermarkets):
- High profile products are priced aggressively.
- Low profile products have much higher mark ups.

Put prices up and then reduce them as 'half price offers' – and maybe even do this as a full time way of doing business (has anyone ever purchased a full price sofa from a furniture discount store?).

Make stock unique so no one can compare our prices.

Publish cheap prices deals to lure customers like moths to a flame, but make these less valuable when the customer looks into the details.

The 'Slow Selling' countertype

Keep slowly giving **genuine value without compromising on quality at every point of contact.**

Never complicate pricing to hoodwink the customer: they won't be hoodwinked in the long term!

If you win a customer on a 'special offer' or 'cut price deal', then you'll lose them just as quickly to your competitors on similar deals.

Case study:

- Lidl and Aldi: the 'no frills' supermarket chains that consistently offers very high quality and genuinely competitive prices (NOT special offers!). These supermarkets are enjoying continual market share growth, even in tough markets.

Limited guarantees

'Speedy Selling' Processes

Limit guarantees: they're only there to give a customer some security so they buy from us, but, in reality we've covered ourselves so carefully that it'll be 'harder than it's worth for them to call us to account' on it.

The 'Slow Selling' countertype

Don't limit guarantees: make them open and transparent and promote them in everything you do.

If one of your customers isn't happy, you don't want them to tell anyone else, you want them to tell you so you can put it right before they leave.

Be remarkable! Blow them away with your caring and genuine response to feedback, complaints and your guarantee.

Slow Tip:

Offer comprehensive, no quibble guarantees.

Train and empower everyone in how to deal effectively with complaints (blow the customer's socks off) at first point of contact

Case study:

- Abel & Cole the Organic Box home delivery retailers have an amazing guarantee system. They understand the value of reputation and referrals. They've taken the time to think through their response to any feedback, they've trained and empowered their people brilliantly, and they've put their money where their mouth is. If you ever need to contact them, they will systematically blow you away with their caring and generous responses. They are a company with hordes of raving fans as customers.

Part 5:
Selling Actions

'An ounce of action is worth a ton of theory'.

> Gandhi

'What you do speaks so loudly that I cannot hear'.

> Ralph Waldo Emerson.

Opening techniques

'Speedy Selling' Processes

- In your face
- Over enthusiastic
- Great offers
- Hype
- An example on Linked in we received recently:
    Hi! Just wanted to say a big THANK YOU for taking the time to add me as a connection. DO check out my website and blogs for lots of FREE tips and tricks to boost your business performance. Here is another FREE heads up, does your LinkedIn profile look like a resume!? Take a look at my summary and how I'm using it as a way to SELL the services of XXXXXX. LinkedIn is the Worlds No.1 B2B social network so if that is your market make sure it is working for you! Regards

The 'Slow Selling' countertype

Slow down … Follow the techniques set out above: Open with genuine questions and genuine expressions and offers of love and value.

Slow Tip:

Aim to build 'remarkability' from the start by adding significant value up front.

Offer valuable information that will empower them to make great decisions, and aim to be remarkable by being a contact / relationship of value whether they buy something from you today or not. So: a 'win/win' or 'no thanks today' for the right reasons.

Case study:

- Credit safe is a leading provider of Company Credit Reports. They aim to 'change the way business information is used by providing high quality data in an easy to use format, allowing everyone in an organisation to make smarter business decisions'.
- One of their truly GREAT 'opening techniques' has been to publish and make available, free of charge, a simple, easy to understand booklet called 'Getting Paid for Dummies'. It's a wonderful piece of work, adds massive long-term value to customers current and potential, and builds a relationship of uncompromising trust before a customer has even committed to engaging with them. Genius!

E-Marketing

'Speedy Selling' Processes

The shotgun approach: it's easy and cheap to buy huge lists and send out lots of offers … so we do!

Spam and rubbish:
- 'Did you get my last email?'
- A special offer for you Guy to help you save money!
- Only a few spaces left!
- Last reminder email …

The 'Slow Selling' countertype

Slow down … Avoid e-marketing altogether. Go instead for loyalty, reputation and referrals by 'e-helping'. Yes, of course you probably need a web presence and to be active on social media, but perhaps you could best use these avenues to engage people, educate, add value and deliver add-on services to customers and potential customers.

Slow Tip:

Avoid e-marketing: instead, focus on e-helping

By systematically blowing your customers' socks off, you don't need to give silly offers away using mass e-marketing techniques, no matter how cheap or easy it is. Instead you can grow continually, quickly and sustainably by:

- ✓ Your customers wanting to come back and buy more frequently.
- ✓ Your customers cross purchasing and up-buying.
- ✓ New customers coming to you by continual direct recommendation.

✓ New customers hearing about you indirectly and contacting you because of your well-spread reputation.

> **Case study:**
>
> - A small Accountancy Business we helped, some years ago, stopped giving special deals to tempt new customers, and instead adopted the ideas and systems outlined in this book. They focused on helping and adding value to their customers in any way they could: one thing they did was to change their e-marketing to e-helping, by circulating top tips and ideas to make their clients' lives easier (and never sharing anything that didn't do this). By doing all this they have found they can sustainably grow by 20 – 30% every year whilst cutting marketing costs to almost nil!

Demonstrate capability

'Speedy Selling' Processes

Strong marketing, supported by a plethora of sales techniques to persuade customers of our capability.

It also helps if we can sponsor something that 'looks good' so we 'get our name out there'.

Testimonials on our website help make us look good.

The 'Slow Selling' countertype

The principle of karma: No one gives a damn about you and your name: they just want to know what you're like and whether you'll be able to help them with their needs.

Be remarkable by focusing on the customer's REAL needs and position yourself to help them whether they buy from you or not: as we've stated repeatedly!

Remember, EVERY physical transaction is driven by an emotional need. This emotional need will ALWAYS be a mix of the following 3 principles:

Slow Tip:

Find out the customers' REAL needs (through onion peeling and feedback).

Continually develop and improve your offers to address these REAL needs.

- ✓ Trust: are you both competent and considerate?

- ✓ Easier/Better Life: do you physically and emotionally make the customer's life easier or better?
- ✓ Attention: does the customer feel like you GENUINELY care in all that you do? Directly and indirectly?

Focus on the customer and their REAL emotional needs, and this will not only amply demonstrate your capability, but also open up massive new avenues of opportunity for cross and up selling.

Case study:

A wedding photography business:
- A small wedding photography business was struggling to survive because everyone has a super-great camera and video recorder on their phone now: who needs to pay a fortune for a photographer? With us advising them, they looked at their capabilities and how they could add value to their customer in this new, hugely changed, world. Through understanding a new need (an overwhelming number of photos and videos and a need for order and presentation), they started to offer a new service: collecting and collating photos and videos, to make them easy to manage and fun to view. This has resulted in their business more than doubling in size.

Google:
- Google was born at Stanford University, because the exiting search providers were generating inaccurate and biased search results (as they were weighted toward their advertisers). The REAL need was for a search engine that was quick, accurate and above all, unbiased. When Google did this successfully, their reputation spread like wildfire, first across University campuses, then across the world. They demonstrated capability amply by simply focusing on the customer and their REAL needs … not by marketing and advertising!

Probe

'Speedy Selling' Processes

Techniques that probe the customer, to create desire or fear (where it wasn't before) by manipulating them.

The 'Slow Selling' countertype

Have an organised process to help the customer slow down, understand the issues, consider the plusses and minuses and make a good decision, whether they buy from you or not.

The slow selling system, as already outlined, will deliver exactly this: work together constructively to get a win/win agreement … or no deal today (where we have a relationship of mutual trust and support but we agree on this occasion that we cannot help you … but we have established such a good reputation in your mind that you'd unhesitatingly come back to us in the future and in the meantime happily recommend us to your friends).

Slow Tip:

Don't probe: instead, slow down, and help the customer by uncovering their REAL needs (they often didn't know them themselves before you did your professional slow selling).

Case study:

A professional services Organisation:

- It's 'expensive' to hire a coach, and few Organisations are keen to sign on the dotted line without seeing what the coaching organisation can do.
- So, in order to address this very real problem, and genuinely put the client's mind at rest, we offer an introductory 'Business Surgery' service: this service looks at every aspect of the Organisation, mostly through the eyes of the teams working there, and produces a detailed picture of the current situation, with proposals for development.
- While this is a chargeable service (at fixed and transparent rates), it is also covered by our no quibble guarantee (the client only pays what they think the work was worth). So they can get a full picture and plan with complete peace of mind, and the relationship quickly develops real value, without messing around with 'free initial consultancy' offers and the like.

Give demonstrations / send proposals

'Speedy Selling' Processes

Customers want details presentations and proposals (and glossy brochures), particularly when it's a significant investment being made.

The 'Slow Selling' countertype

Take it slowly, get it right for the long term.

You're often wasting both your time and energy when you give detailed presentations and produce glossy brochures (they don't even light the fire very well!).

If you need to gloss it up substantially in order to sell it, then perhaps it isn't that great in the first place and you'd maybe be better advised to spend this time and money in improving it rather than polishing it?

Instead, be remarkable in slow steps: work with the customer to explore the customer's real needs and how any proposed solution will affect them, short, medium and long term. Use the win/win sales process to do this and then (and only then) confirm the outcomes (whether and what you have or have not agreed) in the form of a win/win written agreement.

> **'No Deal Today'**
>
> 'No deal today' is fine for the right reasons: **the only crime with 'no deal today' is to make it needlessly time consuming or expensive** by not following the Slow Selling steps properly.

Large presentations and proposals will always be full of holes, and the buyer can and will rip them apart / find reasons to squeeze you on price, latch on to minor objections and pick and choose from the whole (usually ending in a sub optimal outcome for both parties which ends in dissatisfaction and recrimination): don't allow this to happen – build the relationship of mutual trust and mutual benefit first using the slow selling processes … the long term win/win sales will follow.

Be prepared for 'no deal today' in any situation: you can get a 'no deal' for two valid reasons:

- ✓ A 'no deal today': where you've done everything right, built a relationship of mutual trust and mutual benefit, but you've both agreed that a 'no sale today' is the right outcome for now.
- ✓ A 'no deal at all': where you both agree (or you decide on your own) that you're not the right supplier for this customer … (or that this customer is firmly fixed in the old -fashioned 'speedy seller / difficult buyer' mindset and won't move).

Case study:

- A complementary health practice asked us to come in and give a presentation to all the partners on customer service and loyalty. We didn't think this was an effective and valuable way to help them, so we discussed this suggestion in a win/win way and eventually agreed to have two full days in their venues, listening to the partners, the practitioners and the assistants, and then to turn this into a detailed strategic report for them to either implement on their own, or employ us to help them with.
- They agreed to a fair fee for this work, and were assured of their complete peace of mind by our value for money guarantee. We went on to work with them for many years following this start.

Slow Tip:

Slow down: especially with large purchases or B2B relationships: work with the customer as a trusted adviser to find out their REAL needs in the short, medium and long term.

This is much more valuable than any proposal or glossy brochure. (These may also be needed, but only AFTER the trusted adviser work).

Close

'Speedy Selling' Processes

ABC – 'Always be closing'.
Use all the techniques and tools you can learn to always 'close a sale' as quickly and efficiently as you can.

The 'Slow Selling' countertype

The principle of win/win: ABH - 'Always be Helping'
If you stick to this all customers (actual and potential) will see you as a trustworthy and helpful supplier, and, when they want what you supply, will tend to buy from you as first choice: you don't need to 'sell' to them, they will want to buy from you!

However, you can't be naïve: you need organised, customer focused sales journeys that bring the interaction to a decision (as we discussed earlier): you're looking for the decision of 'yes please' or 'not today thanks' for the right reasons!

Case study:

A B2B drinks supplier:
- A B2B drinks supplier we work with offers training and support to pubs and hotels, whether they are direct customers or not. By doing this, they add massive value to their market as a whole, continually build their reputation, and, by the way, continually build their own business and win new customers.

Closing techniques

'Speedy Selling' Processes

- The assumptive: the salesperson intentionally assumes that the prospect has already agreed to buy, and wraps up the sale. "Just pass me your credit card and I'll get the paperwork ready."
- Alternative: ask a question like 'would you like a red one or a blue one?' before the customer has agreed to buy.
- The Sharp Angle: if I can [do a deal], would you be willing to commit today?
- Why: a particularly annoying repetition of 'why' until you can get to the sharp angle close.
- Limited offer: puts pressure on the customer to commit today.
- Last chance: similarly ramps up the pressure.
- Order form fill in: you fill in the order form as you are talking and then ask them to sign at the bottom.
- Negative yes: too manipulative and involved to describe slowly.
- Reduction to ridiculous: where you reduce the issues so they are tiny over the full lifetime of the product or service, or compared to the clear benefits the sale will produce. [*Note: if done with integrity, as part of the in depth understanding of the bigger picture, this approach can be fine, but not if done with a hidden agenda*].
- Lost sale: act as if you're about to leave, so the customer relaxes, then ask 'Where did I go wrong? What stopped you from buying?' [*Note: again, if done with integrity, as part of relationship building, this could be ok, but not as a manipulative 'closing technique'*]
- And there are plenty more! We Googled 'Closing Techniques' while researching, this and got 7.3 million results: you have a lot to choose from!)

The 'Slow Selling' countertype

The principle of proactivity and the 'golden rule' apply: slow down, always own the next step, and get agreement from the customer as to what suits them best. Help the customer move forward slowly towards an optimum solution today, by employing all the slow selling techniques we've discussed, and gently moving them along to a concrete decision.

Remember the golden rule: always treat others as you would want to be treated if you were them in this situation.

You are both looking for a concrete DECISION … today … to agree the next steps and avoid wasting time and effort … NOT A CLOSE!

The only 'sub optimal' decision is where there is 'no decision' (so very little of value has been achieved by either party), or where you get a yes or no decision for the 'wrong' reasons.

Make sure you've made a 'slow selling contract' up front, with the clear Intent (win/win or no deal today) and Desired Results (both parties gave and received true value), then work together to get the right outcome that fulfils these.

This is sometimes called the 'Winston Churchill Approach': meaning that Mr Churchill used to carefully weigh up, in list form, the pros and cons of any action: then, dispassionately, he could make a sensible decision based on the evidence and impact of the options. This can be a good way to describe the 'slow selling contract' that you aim to put in place up front with your customer.

Slow Tip:

Never leave without a decision (it's of no value to anyone if you do).

Always take ownership of the next step (your role is to make the customer's life easier, remember!)

Case study:

- A premium Kitchen retailer we worked for was struggling with finding the 'right' customers for their top end kitchens, and was suffering a very low conversion ('close') rate for any surveys and quotes they did. We advised them, similarly to the kitchen retailer we have already mentioned, to change their process from 'trying to sell' to 'trying to help the customer make the right decision for them, whether they buy from us or not'.
- Doing this properly automatically filtered out them doing surveys and quotes where they were never going to get the business, gave them hugely more confidence in their product and systems, allowed them to relax and be themselves, so the potential customers trusted them more (so they attracted more interest from the more suitable type of customer), and increased their conversion rate (by just following a 'helping' rather than 'selling' process) by almost 40%.

Get a commitment

'Speedy Selling' Processes

Get the customer to commit to something or move on to the next customer (stop wasting time!).

The 'Slow Selling' countertype

There's nothing wrong with getting a commitment provided it's done in the right way for the right reasons.

You're the professional here: you should always own and direct the process. Take the time to sell slowly and professionally: customers want their life to be easier and less stressful by dealing with you. You own the next move and you discover what it should be in order to get a win/win outcome (or no deal today).

Be remarkable as a non-negotiable principle, and keep a relationship open … because situations can change in the future.

You then stick to the next move, through a strong belief of wanting to be remarkable and add value to the relationship no matter what, whether they buy from you today or not.

Slow Tip:

- Use the 'Slow Selling sales process' to make sure you have a win/win relationship with your customer.
- Have an up-front agreement to go for 'win/win' or 'no deal today' no matter what.
- Agree a follow up process that benefits the customer (and helps you learn, grow and win the customer's loyalty as a side benefit)

Example done poorly

- A Chalet Holiday Company we were customers of, never bothered to contact us after the holiday in any way, or to gather feedback properly (and it was NOT a cheap holiday!), but they were all over us like a rash with offers and brochures at the start of the next season. We browsed their offer but weren't wowed and therefore decided to look elsewhere. They then bombarded us with systematic emails (all of which were annoying rather than persuasive in any way), but they never phoned to chat. If they had done, we probably would have booked with them again: as it was we went with another Company (who we have since rebooked with). £000's of business lost all for the sake of a well-executed phone call!

Case study:

- A credit check Company we work with, have excellent, customer focused, win/win communication systems, whereby they follow up and agree next steps with regards: incomplete forms, inactive contacts and lapsed customers. This is done in a helpful collaborative way – not in a salesy way – and they enjoy Industry leading conversion rates and continual sales growth by generating and never deviating from the Mission: To always care about getting it right.

Leading questions

'Speedy Selling' Processes:

- **Questions to lead the customer towards purchasing.**
- **Questions to promote fear and uncertainty and unrealistic aspirations (as outlined above).**

The 'Slow Selling' countertype

Slow down, ask open

> **Slow Tip:**
>
> Use up front agreements and open questions to get to 'win/win' or 'no deal today' no matter what.

> **Slow Tip:**
>
> Use up front agreements and open questions to get to 'win/win' or 'no deal today' no matter what.

questions to genuinely 'peel the onion' and build relationships to get to a mutually beneficial outcome as expediently as possible: no one wants to waste time, but no one wants to make poor decisions more. Act in haste… repent at leisure!

Outcomes we want to generate are:

Win/win
> They buy now for the right reasons.

No Deal today
> They don't buy now for the right reasons.

We always want to avoid

Win /lose
> They buy for the wrong reasons (and we risk getting strung up by their reviews, returns, complaints and buyer's remorse).

Lose/win
> We don't get the sales we should be getting because we didn't do the job properly, so we'll be uncompetitive and struggle to remain in business (and this is a LOT more common than you might think!).

Case study:

- A quality brand car dealership we helped had spent over £100k on a new flashy showroom, but had not received any perceived improvement in sales and revenue as a result …
- We helped them change their entire approach, from website, to phone systems, to reception to execution. Focusing on adding value through quality questions and well trained, customer focused people. Within a year of adopting this approach, their service department had registered at 30% plus increase in sales, and reinvigorated over 250 lapsed customers!

I have 6 honest serving men,
They serve me good and true:
Their names are 'what', and 'how' and 'when'
And 'why' and 'where' and 'who'.

                                                    Rudyard Kipling

Open and closed questions

'Speedy Selling' Processes

Open questions to build a relationship quickly, and closed questions to move the customer to sale or no sale today quickly.

So we need a list of specific questions that we've thought up in advance, and we need to practice using these at every opportunity to get the customer closer to the sale. These questions are specifically designed to help us close the sale quickly and efficiently.

The 'Slow Selling' countertype

Use open questions 90% of the time to build relationships.

Closed questions only when these are genuinely helpful to the customer, to clarify and enumerate what has or hasn't been agreed and what will happen next etc.

We never have a list of questions thought up in advance, and we never have any hidden agendas or clever processes aimed at getting a closure as quickly as possible: our authentic and a single intent from questions is to operate the slow selling process as well as possible, in order to know how the customer feels, what they genuinely want to achieve, and how we can help them best, whether we sell to them today or not…

Case study:

- We worked with a parts retailer for vintage cars and bikes. We help them set up a YouTube and a Facebook process aimed at helping their target customers build and mend their vintage vehicles as effectively as possible. The authentic and single intent from these systems was to generate a powerful, helpful resource that they could use to solve their problems, whether they used our client or not.
- Of course, we found that the better they did this and the more resources they made available free of charge and without any obligation, the more new customers they won and the more sales they made.

Slow Tip:

Use open questions and 'onion peeling' techniques at all stages in the process to add value... whether they buy from you today or not.

Closing

'Speedy Selling' Processes

Closing is the key to selling: all staff need to be taught and pressured into closing more.

Slow Tip:

Only 'close' when you genuinely feel you've reached a win/win outcome: never close a win/lose!

Always agree and own the 'next step': remember you're building a relationship and trying to make the customer's life easier, whether they buy from you today or not...

The 'Slow Selling' countertype

Slow down! Only close when you have reached a clear win/win through great questioning and relationship systems: then it won't feel like closing anyway, it'll be a genuine win/win!

Be OK with 'no deal' today as long as you have built trust and attention and been generally 'remarkable' (the customer will reward you for this by coming back later and in the meantime promoting you to their friends).

Never close a win/lose deal: tell the customer: if you're not sure the customer is making the best decision (because you have more information than they do), say something like: 'I have a concern ... I am not sure this is right because ....' Then work together to get a win/win or no deal today.

Case study:
- We worked with a large commercial cleaning franchise. They do a wonderful job for large clean-ups and commercial situations, but they can be expensive compared to their competition in the 'ad hoc' domestic market (and this had caused bad reviews, lapsed customers and payment problems in the past). In this situation, they are now trained to mention that:
    - They would be delighted to do the job.
    - They guarantee to give the best results available (they have the best and most powerful equipment on the market).
    - There are cheaper options available.
    - They offer a monthly low-cost maintenance solution (which may suit them better).
    - What would the customer like them to do?
- Taking these actions significantly increased customer conversion, retention and referral rates, and eliminated bad reviews and payment problems from these customers!

Cold calling

'Speedy Selling' Processes

No one really likes cold calling, but it can be a necessary evil when you need to sell things. Anyway, these days you can employ people cheaply all over the world to do the telephoning for you: after all, if you achieve enough volume, cheaply enough, the bottom line comes through positive at the end of the day.

We do a 'big push' on sales calling in quiet times when we need to drum up trade.

We'll bombard people with 'Amazing special offers' and 'we're in your area at the moment' marketing offers … how could they say 'no'?!

The 'Slow Selling' countertype

Go slower! Cold calling is intrinsically anti-social: in the age of the empowered consumer, people now have a choice, and they can find you and your competitors, what you sell and what 'the word on the street' is about you, at the drop of a hat.

You should only cold call if you are genuinely imparting valuable information (such as a new product or service to the area), and it should be done in an informative / relationship building / ok with 'not now' way.

Take it slowly, if you have to do it at all (it is of course far better to base your customer acquisition and sales growth system on a 'slow selling' system), and follow these rules:

- Focus on sound foundations of customer reputation and loyalty first... don't DO ANY MARKETING AT ALL UNTIL YOU'VE GOT THIS RIGHT ... THERE'S NO POINT (the potential customers can dig the dirt on you too easily).
- Quality leaflets with well-designed information hold more value to recipients (people just delete emails).
- It's worthwhile taking the time and making the effort to explain VERY simply and clearly the key advantages of your system honestly, who it's most suited to and who it isn't, and tell them you'll be calling in this timescale to follow this up, and this is your number (and address) if they want to call you or they want you to take them off your list.
- Make it VERY easy for the customer to say 'No thanks, not today': it's madness not to!
- The aim should be to build long term customers because your system / approach and 'genuineness' are better …. NOT to hoodwink the lazy/ignorant into saying 'yes' because they haven't done their homework.

You may perhaps want to run an event to add value, so the customer can size you up at no risk and significant benefit (this works very well for B2B situations) … but make sure there is NO SELLING at this event: just add massive value, inform them what you can do to help, give them easy ways to

Slow Tip:

Make sure any 'cold' communication carries intrinsic value to the recipient … whether they do business with you today or not.

follow up, outline your easy low cost 'start up' services, and perhaps even have an opt in for you to call them for feedback after the event.

This feedback should comply with the general rules of feedback as we explain elsewhere in this book:

- Feedback first: this is the prime aim, to help you improve your events so as to make them more effective and productive for both parties in the future.
- Then, and only then, can you ask:
    - If they think the event was 'great': 'Would you like to start trying our services?' (in whatever guise this would be for your business).
    - If they think the event was 'OK': 'What would we need to do to get you to try our services at some time in the future?'
    - If they think the event was 'Poor': 'What could we have done differently to make it better?'
        - Are they simply not our target customer, or are they a target customer who we have got off on the wrong foot with? The answer to this will dictate the action you then take.

Make sure you comply with the law (the fact that the laws across the world are tightening up significantly indicates what customers think of cold calls in general).

Follow up as you say you will (reliability is key, as they don't know you yet).

Be sure not to pester: assume a low success rate and make sure this is profitable (in the long term) before you start (or don't do it).

Case study:
- We worked with a large Business Banking team who struggled to get new customers in a crowded, deal driven market. They developed a system to stand out from the crowd by offering high value workshops and short training sessions, using local experts. The experts are chosen for their genuine value (not their self-promotion prowess!), and there is no 'selling' allowed.
- The Bank's customers are all invited, and can bring a guest each, and they open extra spaces to 'cold invited' local businesses. This process not only wins the Bank new customers, over the long term, but also adds significant value to the relationship with existing customers … as well as being beneficial to the speakers / trainers (they get introduced to quality businesses who may need their services).

Email selling / PPC / Targeted Ads

'Speedy Selling' Processes:
- Volume, done cheaply will pay off.
- 'Amazing special offers' which rarely are!
- Bombard big lists to look like we're doing our job.
- Use clever phrases to get people to click
- Embellish the offer to create 'clickbait'
- Target ads closely and use funnels to get the customer to come to you.
- You know the score, it happens every day!

Slow Tip:

Treat others as you'd like to be treated if you were them: only ever send out something that you'd genuinely like to receive.

The 'Slow Selling' countertype

Cold e-marketing is intrinsically anti-social, for the same reasons as cold calling: it's a sad indictment on our society that one of the most useful and valuable communication systems, email and the web, has been made significantly more time-consuming and less effective due to the widespread misuse by the 'speedy selling' types…

Any sales achieved through any (even minor) form of misinformation, smoke and mirrors or truth embellishment, will be short term at best, and disastrous for the long term at worst. Don't rush to use 'the latest sexy tool that will drive an avalanche of customers to you while you sleep'.

Take it slowly: just because it's a sexy tool, won't make you an attractive proposition. By all means use the latest tools, and put significant effort into proper focusing and proper understanding of the customer's real needs, but always defer to focus on sound foundations of customer reputation and loyalty first.

Explain what the e marketing will and won't do: focus on:

- ✓ Mission: Adding value to the relationship (because you have information that's valuable and worth the customer knowing about).
- ✓ Customer's REAL Needs: make them short, easy to read, laid out in a clear and interesting manner and with genuine value.
- ✓ Go the Extra inch: add value in short bursts, share information from others that'd be genuinely valuable to your customer, only add links for the customer to follow or buy from when you're 100% convinced that it's genuinely adding value (and make sure that emails with 'buying messages' in them are very much in the minority).
- ✓ Measure: put in 'lead measures' to see what gets responded to well, and what doesn't.

In other words, keep it simple, do it well.

Case study:

- Seth Godin. Seth Godin is one of the most successful and influential business writers in the world. His books sell by the hundreds of thousands (in a hugely crowded marketplace) and his training courses sell out in a few hours. Why? Because, through his wonderful daily blog, he systematically adds massive value every day to all his recipients, whether they buy from him or not.
- https://en.wikipedia.org/wiki/Seth_Godin

Electronic 'Smart' Selling

'Speedy Selling' Processes

Technology allows us to do things we've never done before online: we can follow up un checked out baskets, we can create pop-up adverts depending on location and browsing history, and we can manipulate our prices and offers depending on potential customer behaviour.

The 'Slow Selling' countertype

Natural principles are king: yes, you can do lots of smart and exciting stuff by using new technology – and it'll only get better – but the fundamental seller/customer relationship remains the same. Human emotions haven't changed, no matter how fast and 'smart' technology becomes. If you try clever tricks that are not driven by clear principles of genuineness, trustworthiness and real value, your sales drives will be like a house of cards. As soon as the customers find out how you've been hoodwinking them, they'll never trust you again, play you at the same game, and vigorously shop around on price. The result will be a lose/lose race to the bottom where buying and selling becomes unnecessarily complicated and wasteful for both parties … and the market becomes ripe for the entry and takeover of a new business that IS conforming with the slow selling principles.

Case study:

Easy Jet:
- Easy Jet created a 'new', and very profitable, market of frequent short haul flying, by focusing on no frills, simple clear great value pricing, and obsessive delivery on what they promised. Through this they gained customer trust and continual growth in sales.
- (Of course, not everyone likes the Easy Jet approach to business: but they fundamentally changed their market and created a large and profitable business in what was already considered to be a 'saturated' situation).

Sales & Discounts

'Speedy Selling' Processes

Discounts and 'special offers' drive volume. Offer discounts to attract new customers only: don't make these available to existing customers (it's a waste of money).

Example: Most Phone / Bank / Insurance packages.

A great tool to use is to 'Make discounts up / have made up 'sales'' (i.e. put the price up first, or publish list prices that are way higher than the normal market rate, then publish 'amazing discounts' and 'this week only special offers', so the customer thinks they're getting a bargain.

Example: 'Discount' furniture retailers who always have a 'sale on' (please note: this CAN be a reasonable model for a successful business, provided the following three conditions are met:

Slow Tip:

Treat short-term sexy tools with caution.

Stick to your principles in all you do... no exceptions, no matter how cool the tool is.

1. Your products are unique and cannot be genuinely compared with your competitors' on the open market.

2. Your products are actually of good quality (a bad reputation will outblast any marketing, no matter how large the budget, just look at the case of 'Ratners, the Jewellers' for proof of this).
3. You NEVER stop promoting this process: it's like a bicycle: if you stop pedalling hard, you'll fall off!

Slow Tip:

- Be real with offers and discounts.
- Use them as a reward for loyalty rather than as a bait for new custom.
- Develop value in your customer loyalty club that will get people keen to join.

The 'Slow Selling' countertype

It's true that everyone loves a bargain, so some discounts are a very good idea: eg

- ✓ Discounts for volume.
- ✓ Discounts for slow/old stock clearance.
- ✓ Genuine special events.

But you need to slow down and **stick to being real**: it's the only long-term option (as stated above: if you trade in an 'unreal' way you have to keep this up forever or you immediately go out of business when you stop).

Tell all your existing customers of any deals / offers up front and before anyone else and make it as easy as possible for them to take advantage of them (no matter how much more profitable it might be for you to keep quiet about them).

Case study:

- We worked with a Brewer, who was struggling to compete against continual 'special offers' from competitors.
- After spending time listening to their customers and the pressures they faced in their market, we helped our client generate a programme of offers and genuine special products (one-off brews etc) that would only be available to existing loyal customers. These were very good offers and the extent and availability depended on the customers' loyalty record.
- The net result of this activity has been a significant upturn in customer loyalty, combined with a significant increase in new customers (wanting to be part of this privileged group)!

Free!

'Speedy Selling' Processes

'Free' is the magic word: we can then take advantage of the customer lowering their guard and then tie them into a purchase whether it's in their best interest or not.

> E.g.: garage: 'Free winter health check': the customer is then led on to buying add ons they may or may not need or want, through fear or obligation.

'Free' gets people to buy more than they would otherwise.

> E.g.: supermarket: BOGOF is a better deal that '50% off'.

If we throw in extra stuff 'for free', then customers will feel good about us.

> E.g.: 'I'll throw in some free car mats with that' when you buy a new car.

The 'Slow Selling' countertype

Be real: do things slower: nothing is really 'free': it's factored into the price somewhere. If it's 'too good to be true' it probably is: customers who buy things because of 'free' offers are disloyal and untrustworthy: they're loyal to the offer, not to the brand! If your business is dependent on attracting these types of people, you're quickly on the way to going out of business.

The world is awash with 'free' offers, and customers have been caught out in the past far too often, so they intrinsically mistrust these 'offers' and will act with caution (unless they are the above customers who are only loyal to the offer: and you don't want these customers anyway!).

Trust and slow selling is more important than quick offers: if you want to give 'free' offers to get attention and create action from a customer, then do it slowly and honestly, and make it a genuine win/win deal.

For example:
- If you run a garage and offer a 'free winter health check', give a guaranteed outcome of one of 3 things:
  1. No issues at all.
  2. Some minor issues with a quote, and timescale, for the work, which you can take away and compare or consider.
  3. Some major issues with a quote, which you can take away and consider

     (Sure, some 'customers' will take advantage of you if you do this, but, (and it's a BIG but), these are the customers you DON'T want (hooray, they've gone elsewhere … just remember to turn them away in the future), AND, by doing this kind of offer, you will attract more people, increase conversion rates, and build loyalty and reputation at the same time. The customers who take advantage of you should be seen as the 'marketing cost of getting it right'!)
- If you run a retail business: be up front and transparent with all prices, focus on high quality first, always offer fair, transparent and competitive prices, and only discount to move specific short-term deals, move ageing stock / make way for new lines:
- If you're in car sales: not only guarantee your rates are the best they'll find in the area, but also make sure that they get all the add-ons that take away all the hassles of getting a new car: e.g.: mats, tune the music system, full fuel, and check-up after a week (and then apply this same thinking to the whole dysfunctional world of car selling).

PRICE

Just a word here on price:
1. If you win a deal on price alone, you'll lose it on price alone
2. People who buy on price alone are often difficult and demanding. They often steal your ideas, and pay late if at all.
3. Customers buy VALUE ... not price: focus on adding VALUE to the experience
4. Great service has a price attached to it ... and, if a customer understands and trusts you, it's often a price they're pleased to pay
5. With Global competition, if your main selling point is price, you're VERY vulnerable
6. Poundland stores got closed by 99p stores so they had to buy the whole company!

Solutions

'Speedy Selling' Processes

Present 'solutions' to customers in your marketing and all subsequent communication.

The 'Slow Selling' countertype

OK, you have a 'possible solution', no more: there is almost always more than one solution to any customer need. So be careful, be modest, take it slowly and talk about possible or alternative solutions, never just 'solutions'. The customer is king and they will tell you what solution they want, not what you want to provide!

> **Slow Tip:**
>
> The REAL 'solution' all customers REALLY want is TEA

Case study:

- Amazon who introduced the different 'buying options' as a standard feature: when they did this, they were universally mocked, but history and results have told their own story, and you know, as a customer, how much you like to be offered alternative solutions by a supplier, with no bias on their part as to what's most profitable to them.
- Guy was buying a wooden front door from a supplier for a holiday cottage refurbishment. The supplier was also supplying a new kitchen. When he discussed the situation in detail (sea front, Atlantic Coast), the salesman said these words:
    - 'I can sell you a really good wooden front door that'll look great, but in that situation, I'd recommend you replace the current wooden door with a UPVC one: it'll look just as good, and last many times longer. We don't sell them, but I can put you in contact with a couple of local firms who I can recommend'
    - So who do you think he will go back to, time and time again, and who will he recommend to anyone who asks him where to buy a door or a kitchen in future? The value of that will be hundreds of times more than the profit in one front door …

Some stats about customer loyalty and retention:

Depending on which study you believe, and what industry you're in, acquiring a new customer is anywhere from five to 25 times more expensive than retaining an existing one. It makes sense: you don't have to spend time and resources going out and finding a new client — you just have to keep the one you have happy. If you're not convinced that retaining customers is so valuable, consider research done by Frederick Reichheld of Bain & Company (the inventor of the net promoter score) that shows increasing customer retention rates by 5% increases profits by 25% to 95%.

https://hbr.org/2014/10/the-value-of-keeping-the-right-customers

After sales techniques

We have already talked about this elsewhere, so I'll keep it as short as possible.

'Speedy Selling' Processes

'After sales' are usually very much an afterthought, if thought about at all.

'After sales' are seen as a 'cost' to be minimised, by:

- Being hard to contact.
- Automating as much as possible.
- Running cheap automated 'customer surveys'.
- No follow up at all.

Example: car sales: in our experience of car buying, when you're interested in buying a car, the sales people are all over you like a rash, but when you've signed on the line, it suddenly becomes very hard to get any attention or help ... unless you're paying for it! (Note: some brands and some dealers DO get it right, but many still don't, we're ashamed to say).

The 'Slow Selling' countertype

Beliefs: The customer has paid us the highest possible compliment by buying our product, so it's a massive opportunity to now develop this into great levels of loyalty, reputation and referrals ... and it's so cheap and easy to do: all we need is good well thought through systems, backed up by a little proper effort, and we can have a massive impact!

> **Remember:** it takes a lifetime to build a reputation and minutes to destroy it. This is not a business feature which is "nice to have"; in today's market this feature is a "must have" for survival.

Emotions: 'After sales' is not a cost, it's a massive investment in loyalty, reputation and referrals: the better we do it, the better return we'll get. The return is at least 5X greater than any marketing spend in getting new customers.

Actions:

Change the names

- ✓ **'After sales' could change to 'Future sales' or 'Loyal Customer Relationships'.**
- ✓ **'Customer Service' could change to 'Customer Experience'.**
- ✓ **'Sales' could change to 'Purchases' (and this changes everything, including the title of this book).**
- ✓ **'Selling' could change to 'buying'.**

Slow Tip:

Treat repeat customers better than new ones.

Always aim to attract new customers because existing ones rave about how remarkable you are.

Put in place continual improvement systems, using customer feedback.

Results: the upturn in results will be a slow burn (this is after all 'Slow Selling'!), but when it starts, it'll continue, and it'll grow and grow and grow, while your marketing costs shrink and shrink and shrink.

Case study:

We worked with a quality car dealer network and set up with them the following system:

- Changed the belief and emotions from: 'Our cars are amazing, people will come to us if they want one', to 'We're here to be more amazing than our brand, so that anyone wanting a quality car in this area wouldn't think twice about only coming to see us'.
- Actions:
    - Set up slow sales systems.
    - Changed the name of their 'After Sales' dept to their 'Loyal Customer Relationship' department.
    - Introduced a 'blow their socks off' after sales system for car purchasers and car servicing.
    - Introduced a 'blow their socks off' feedback and reaction system.
- Result = customer spend and happiness increased to top 10% in their market.

A good example of an after sales communication, I received the same day as writing this section from Virgin Wines:

Hi there,

Thanks for buying our wines!

You have found the very best place to buy wine in the UK – we've just been voted **Online Drinks Retailer Of The Year** and we're very proud!

It means we are **officially** the best place to buy wine – but we knew that already!

I hope you enjoy the wines delivered today. Every wine in our range is there because we think it deserves its place. Exclusive. Independent. And of the very highest quality.

But I need your help. What really counts is what you think. Every customer rating counts. On a weekly basis I review the wine ratings, with our team of buyers. It's your ratings that decide which wines make the grade and the style of wines we make with our winemakers.

It also helps all your fellow customers make a decision on the wines they might like to try. We don't edit or remove any reviews (no naughty words allowed though!), so you can be sure it's an honest view of what our customers think about the wines.

Please take the opportunity to review the wines you have chosen and remember if you do, we'll add a free bottle into the next case you order. It's our way of saying "thanks" for your help.

To place a review, simply log on to your account, find the wines you've bought in your order history and let us know what you think.

Also within this envelope you'll find some special offers from our friends and partners. I hope you find something of interest.

I'm always here and keen to receive your feedback, good or bad. Please do get in touch by email on jay@virginwines.co.uk or come and say hi at our next wine tasting event.

I'm hugely confident about the quality of our wines and I can guarantee they knock the socks off the boring plonk available elsewhere. I put my money where my mouth is too with a 100% enjoyment guarantee so please, let us know if any fail to impress. If you like the wines as much as I think you will, please tell your friends – it's always nice to share the love!

Cheers

Jay

Jay Wright

Life's too short for boring wine!

Virgin Wines, The Loft, St. James' Mill, Whitefriars, Norwich, NR3 1TN

This is fabulous! Open and friendly, direct, simple, rewarding and with personal commitment from the MD by name, with his contact details included!

Getting referrals and introductions

'Speedy Selling' Processes

- The 'Machine Gun Approach': if we shout loudly enough to everyone, someone will refer us
- The 'Bribery Approach':
    - If we offer $250 for a successful referral, we're bound to get them aren't we?
- The 'Same Club Approach':
    - If we scratch your back, please will you scratch ours?
- The hoodwink approach: 'leave your business card here for a chance to win a bottle of champagne'

For example: an office space supplier in UK Cities has posters all over the walls (and all over the website), offering £200 cash for successful referrals. But they are always after referrals and new customers … so it can't be working, can it? (If they were doing things according to the 'Slow Selling' approach, we'd expect them to always have a queue, so they'd have no need for the 'bribery approach'!)

The 'Slow Selling' countertype

1. Take it slowly: start by working obsessively on being remarkable: A customer is risking their own personal reputation by referring you: they will only genuinely refer you if you're genuinely referable.
2. And do it properly. The key steps are:
    1. Be genuinely referable (follow all the other steps in this book).
    2. Build the relationship first, then gather feedback.
3. Only ask for referrals from those who tell you you're 'great' through the feedback (for the others, continue to build the relationship until you get to this enhanced state of relationship).
4. Ask if it would be 'OK to ask':

- Say: 'We aim to keep costs down and minimise advertising spend, so we can focus our attention on getting it right. We can see from your feedback that we're currently doing the right things for you. If we asked you, would you be willing to help us contact other organisations / people who might also be pleased to find out what we do?
- If yes: proceed as shown below.
- If no: Ok, we respect that. Will it be OK to ask again in the future (as long as we keep on getting it right for you)?
5. Identify who you want to be referred to and why:
    - Organisations / people who need ABC and want to avoid the hassle of DEF and would genuinely like to talk with an Organisation that does GHI in an XYZ way.
6. Have a great referral system, based on getting referrals by small steps (we call this 'Go the Extra Inch' on referrals).

Stop and work this all through with a 'Raving Fan' group of customers first: they'll tell you what's appropriate, and what isn't!

A 'great' referral system:

Step 1: ask permission to ask for a referral: (as above).

Step 2: ask for it: this is often done by agreeing to:
- Re contact them at an agreed time
- Send them something
- Email them something
- It's usually best not to go straight in at the deep end immediately after asking!

Step 3: thankyou and next steps.
- Direct referral: they agree to contact the referee
- Indirect referral: they give you permission to mention their name to the referee
- Cold referral: they give you contact details / names only and leave it to you

Step 4: contact the referral.

Step 5: have a world class process, based on the 'Slow Selling' principles, to contact the referee.
- (See 'an easy inch by inch process' below)

Step 6: Follow up to get to win/win or no deal. (See processes above).

Step 7: keep the referrer in the loop: they will want to know how you're getting on, after all, they put their reputation on the line to help you. This is vitally important.

Step 8: have a world class, high impact, fun 'thankyou system'.
- Go the extra inch.
- Implement your thank-you system quickly and generously. If it's a genuine referral, <u>even if you don't get any business from it, you should say thank-you with your systems</u>. It shows that, whatever happens, you're genuine and very referable.

Case study:

Regional Solicitors

- We have worked with a regional Solicitor who have focused all systems and processes (and training and measures) on being 'Genuinely Referable'.
- Of course, they aim to be top of their game in competence, but also they aim to be top of the pile in referability.
- We built and implemented a feedback and referral system, by phone, using a 3rd party as an independent implementer, guided by the rules and principles outlined above.
- After 6 months of using this system on a rigorous test basis, they cancelled all other advertising and marketing activity (apart from running high quality free seminars and events focused on educating customers and potential customers), and focused intently on this.
- On average, they have gained one successful referral per 4 jobs on a consistent basis ongoing: a much better conversion rate than ANY marketing, and at a fraction of the cost!

Slow Tip:

- Make 'referrals' a key measure of success.

An easy inch-by-inch approach to approaching a Referee

Here's a step-by-step approach to help you with cold referrals. This is designed for a B2B situation, but you will see that they can be easily adapted to suit any customer relationship. Remember to approach this process in the same way that you do your other calls. Always ask for permission and utilise the inch-by-inch approach.

Step 1: Introduction

Start off a call by giving to the customer you name and the reason for your call. Time is a valuable resource: give them a great reason to spend this valuable resource on you. Always be honest!

Tell them the results you achieved for the referrer. Those results were rated as "great" (otherwise you would not have asked for a referral) so now you have a chance to brag a little bit about it. The referrer would be happy to confirm everything you tell them.

Next is an area where a lot of people really drop the ball. You are not going to be able to help everyone – you have to be honest. Tell them that there might be a way that you can help them get similar results. Don't say that you can definitely help them. How could you possibly know with 100% certainty that you can help them? You don't even know them.

Ask whether this is a good time or if they would prefer that you call them later. You need permission to continue. If it's not a good time, then ask if you can call back at a better time.

You're only going to have a few seconds to earn enough trust to be given permission to continue with the call. Make sure that you craft an introduction that includes everything we mentioned above. This introduction should be between two to three sentences. If you are given permission to continue, then do so. If not, then either reschedule the call or end it. Never try to pitch to anyone who is not interested.

Step 2: Explain Why You Called Them

This one is going to be a value statement based on your customer focused mission. Just be honest and explain exactly what it is that you have to offer.

Make sure you also use this sort of phrase, "our typical customers are those who have a limited budget want to get excellent results without having to spend a fortune."

Step 3: Get Permission to Ask a Genuine Question

You have gone through the introduction and explained what it is that you have to offer. You have their full attention at this point you're going to start peeling the onion.

Lead off with this question:

"Does this seem at all like a product/service that might interest to you?"

Listen to their response closely. When they are finished, then you ask another question. Regardless of their answer being "yes" or "no," respond with this:

"Okay. Can I ask you one question?"

Asking for permission again builds trust and makes them comfortable. It's much better to ask for permission that it is to instantly try selling them something.

Step 4: The Question

The next question depends on their answer to, "Can I ask you one question?"

If they answer yes, ask: "Can I ask what your main issues/opportunities/wants/desires/ pains/problems/needs in this area are and how you solve them at the moment?"

If they answer no, ask: "If I called you back at a better time would you be willing to discuss your main issues or needs in this area, and how you solve them at the moment?"

The trick is to really listen to them, peel the onion gently with open questions. If they tell you "no," then thank them and end the call. It's perfectly okay for them to say no.

Step 5: Get to the Point

By now you will have built up quite a bit of trust. You should also know the problems that they are facing. It's time to get to the point. Work deeply with the customer's real needs. Peel the onion some more.

Here's what you could say:

"I don't want to waste your time and I don't really know yet whether our services might be useful to you. Do you mind if I ask two more questions to determine if it's worth scheduling a more in-depth conversation?"

If they answer "no" then thank them for their time, peel the onion to find out more information if you can – what WOULD they want to talk with you about, now or later – and at the right time, thank them and end the call.

If they answer "yes" then move on to the next step.

Step 6: Ask the Two Questions

Here are the two questions that you ask. Again, make sure that you listen carefully to their response.

"Who are your customers and why do they buy from you as opposed to your competitors?"

This question establishes their current situation.

"What would be the main things you'd like to do better, and what concerns might you have about taking on a new supplier?"

This opens the door as to what they want to know about you.

Step 7: Ending the Call

The end of the call is a very important process that is often overlooked. This is your opportunity to make their life easier, show them attention and build further trust.
Three things must happen at the end of the call.
1. Confirm everything that has been discussed. Then decide what's going to happen next. You can schedule a more in-depth call or even a personal visit. On the other hand, your organization might not be a good fit with theirs. In that case, you absolutely must not try to "make it work." Don't be afraid to say "no."
2. Provide even more value to them by telling them about (genuine) extras that you are able to offer them because they were referred.
3. Genuinely thank them before ending the call. Your goal is to reassure them that they have made a good decision, whatever it is.

Then take it from there with your slow-selling processes.

Overcoming 'Objections' when you approach a referee

That one word 'objection' can seem scary. Well we have some good news for you. The word 'objections' is absolute rubbish. There's no such thing in the business world.

Statements that are seen as objections are, in fact, just genuine concerns from the potential customer for good reasons – primarily about how they can get the best result for themselves.

You would do exactly the same thing if you were in their shoes!

There are concerns that are important, and the action to take is listen, peel and address these legitimate concerns. Whether or not you get a sale is not really important right now. These concerns are paramount.

This is NOT a battle!

Remember your customer focused mission and the customer's real needs. Everything you do should be based on listening and welcoming these concerns. This is the only way that you will ever know how you can genuinely help a customer and build a great long-term relationship so they can in turn refer their contacts to you over time or not.

Remember that no is OK, if you get the relationship right they may want to do business with you later, and refer others to you. Either way, you've not compromised your status of being genuinely remarkable. You've not compromised yourself just to get the sale.

It also reveals the most efficient way to help them.

- Listen deeply. It always seems to come back to listening, doesn't it? That's because so few companies truly listen to their customers. The ones that do are successful.
- Peel the onion with open questions. Make sure that they give you permission to do this.
- Determine their needs and "desired results." It's never about what you want. It's about what they want.
- Only try to solve a problem when they ask you to. Never try solving their problems without permission.
- Work together to find a win/win solution, either you can do business together for the right reasons, or you can't do business together for the right reasons. Never try and do either for the wrong reasons.

And then you'll be fine.

Part 6.
Selling Measures

The Problem

The problem with the world at large and the world of selling in particular is that it is unbalanced ... this is driven by unbalanced measures.

... and **what gets measured gets done** ...

Measures

Measure?

'Speedy Selling' Processes

Measures are based on 'push' activities and are aimed at maximising activity in the misplaced faith that this will in turn maximise sales.

These are usually called 'Lag Measures'.

Example: Insurance sales: many Insurance organisations still base success on 'new customer win numbers' ... (whilst often paying scant attention to numbers of or reasons why customers are lost). This is like continually trying to fill a bucket with a hole in the bottom. The flow rate of the water in it is easy to measure and easy to shout about, but the bottom line 'total water volume' is rarely changing significantly for the better ... and this is surely a much more important number?

The 'Slow Selling' countertype

1. The customer isn't interested in your sales measures and sales targets: they are ONLY interested in their needs.

2. Slow your measures down: focus on the long-term outputs you want, not just the 'immediate sale'. If you measure 'push' actions and results, you will get 'pushy' behaviour: this annoys the customer more than anything else.
3. If you measure 'pull' actions, you'll get pull behaviour and results: 'Slow Selling'.
4. In order to make sure your processes and behaviours are aligned at every level, you MUST have aligned and functional measures, and stick to them, no matter what, through thick or thin.
5. This is MUCH harder than it seems, because all of us have been conditioned by a culture, and hundreds of years of practice, of 'unbalanced measures'. We are conditioned to accepting that, if the purpose of the organisation is to make ever increasing profits, then the only measure that really matters is 'bottom line profit', and therefore we should do anything we can to move this measure in the short term, no matter what happens to other measures.
6. Change the names:
    - 'Sales Measures' could change to 'Purchase Measures'.
    - 'Feedback' scores could be 'Future Success' scores.
    - 'Loyalty' measures might become 'Long term success' measures.

Case study:

Insurance Sales:
- We worked with a standard Regional Insurance Broker, and changed the following actions:
- We helped them:
  - stop measuring obsessively on weekly and daily sales
  - base all systems and processes on the 'Slow Selling' principles
  - start gathering, measuring and incentivising on feedback, loyalty and Customer Experience
  - start rewarding referrals (internally and externally)
- Result = immediate increase of 20% + in business conversion rate, plus customer loyalty rate increased by almost 200% in a year

[Note: we were surprised at how high this figure was. But from our customer feedback we learned that this is a very dysfunctional market, and they didn't expect to be treated well at all. When our client genuinely acted as a 'Slow Seller', it blew their socks off.]

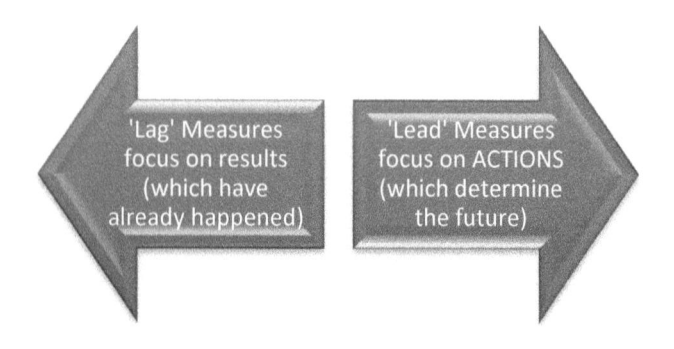

'Lag' Measures focus on results (which have already happened)

'Lead' Measures focus on ACTIONS (which determine the future)

Incentivise

'Speedy Selling' Processes

- Incentivise sales results to drive motivation.
- Incentivise the marketing team to get 'hits' and 'coverage': if we fire enough bullets, we're bound to hit things!
- Have high impact meetings and events to hype people up.
- 'The more we push and shout, the more they'll get off their arses and sell'.

Slow Tip:

Spend a huge amount of time and effort getting your incentives right: this is what drives the everyday behaviour of your people

The 'Slow Selling' countertype

- Put the brakes on: unbalanced incentives produce unbalanced behaviour ... and unbalanced behaviour scares customers off and ruins your reputation.
- Slow down and put balanced sales incentives in place (as set out below): by all means reward success ... but only if you're first success is your reputation for 'remarkability' with your customer.
- Don't incentivise anyone to 'push': 'pushing' produces stress and poor results. Instead, slowly get the right people on the bus, develop remarkable products and support systems, using the 'slow selling' tools, train your people remarkably, incentivise them fairly with balanced incentives, hold them rigorously accountable for results (lead measures first, lag measures to follow), and

continually encourage and praise. Take prompt and fair actions to change those who cannot cope, or move them to a more suitable position inside or outside your organisation.
- Incentivise the marketing department (and everyone) on:
    - Customer happiness.
    - Customer loyalty.
    - Genuine reputation.
- Remember: 'Hits' stands for 'How Idiots Track Success'.

Case study:

Enterprise Rent a Car
- Enterprise has grown from a 1950s start-up (in a crowded market) to the number 1 car rental organisation worldwide: their 'Mission' is 'Take care of your customers and employees first and the profits will follow'.
- All team members are continually monitored and rated on the customer feedback score of their unit and themselves.
- Their promotion processes state that any employee can only be promoted if their customer feedback score is above average (no matter what their skills and talents). That's a major statement and a strong message on incentives.

A short rant on Measures!

What gets measured gets done … right?

Of course.

So, how are sales usually measured?

Usually, by 'sales produced' or 'money'?

Of course.

And, sometimes, by 'activity generated' (which is very often the wrong activity, as discovered above).

So, **what is it that produces those sales?**

As we have found out, it is doing the right things in the right way. So we need some measures of doing the right things in the right way: we call these "**Lead Measures**".

When you want to know what the weather is going to do in the future, you need a barometer that measures the right activities, that will provide you with the right answers in order to take appropriate actions. If it is going to rain, you can choose to stay inside or take an umbrella out with you. If your barometer indicates that it will be sunny, you can take the action of carrying sunglasses and sun cream with you.

In the same way, businesses need a barometer to measure business activities and provide you with the results and answers needed to take appropriate action. This business barometer will provide measures that cannot be manipulated. It simply tells you the plain simple facts of what will happen in the future… Whether you like it or not.

You need to formulate measures within your business in order to take effective and meaningful actions to make sure that you deliver your Customer Focused Mission and delight the customer with their real needs, continually and consistently… No matter what.

So, the solution to Effective Sales Measures is: You need to **discover the key barometric measures in your business**. Measure them continually and obsessively. Have a clear and prominent scoreboard, and make sure these measures are applied at every level of your business so that your employees always know the right steps to take… And then the sales will follow like magic.

For the record

For the record: here is an incomplete list of 'push' or 'lag' measures, that should only be of interest to your finance people:

- Leads generated
- Social media channel usage
- Opportunity to win ratio
- Hits
- Conversion rate
- Sales
- Margin
- Costs
- Profits

And here is an incomplete list of 'pull' or 'lead' measures, that should be the ones you incentivise and measure activity around. Please note the following

- ➢ Some measures are both 'lead' and 'lag' (eg : conversion rates and margin)
- ➢ You need a balanced scorecard that drives the Slow Selling behaviours first, then aligned results second, in order to produce a win/win outcome third.
  - Response rates
  - Response time
  - Rate of contact
  - Rate of follow up
  - Conversion rates
  - Social media channel response rates
  - Marketing collateral
  - Customer feedback

- Margin
- Lapsed customers
- Contact no buy rates
- Contact no buy feedback
- Lapsed customer recovery
- Referrals offered
- 'Thankyous' given
- 'Thankyous' received

Please also note: these measures can and should of course be split / measured by

- Rep
- Channel
- Product
- Depot

In order to hold people / product / and channel individually and independently accountable

Part 7:

Slow Selling:

a simple guide to getting it right

In this section, we set out a simple set of steps and guidelines to 'get it right': this is where all the ideas we've already discussed come together into a logical ordered process, so you can assess your processes and check them off one by one.

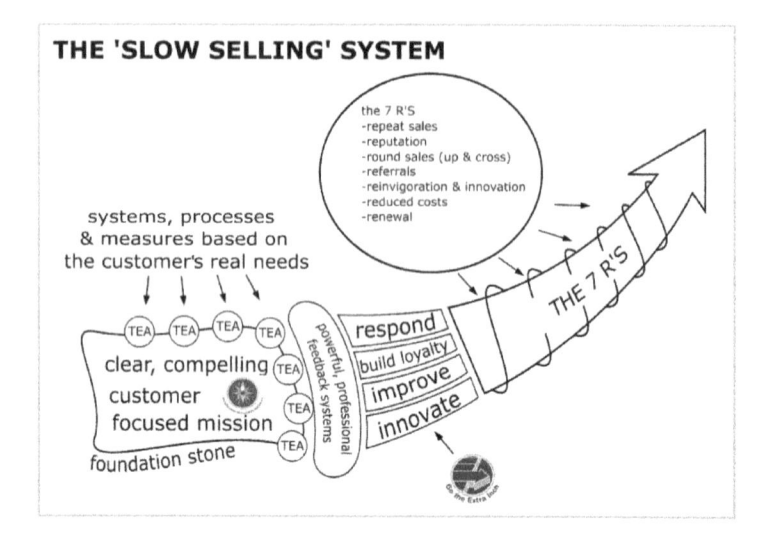

THE 'SLOW SELLING' SYSTEM

the 7 R'S
- repeat sales
- reputation
- round sales (up & cross)
- referrals
- reinvigoration & innovation
- reduced costs
- renewal

systems, processes & measures based on the customer's real needs

clear, compelling customer focused mission

foundation stone

powerful, professional feedback systems

respond
build loyalty
improve
innovate

THE 7 R'S

BELIEFS

Slow Start

Get your mind in the right place first: **you are NOT here to 'make a sale': you are here, as a specialist in your product and market segment, to help the customer**, and be remarkable, whether they end up buying from you today or not. This is non-negotiable.

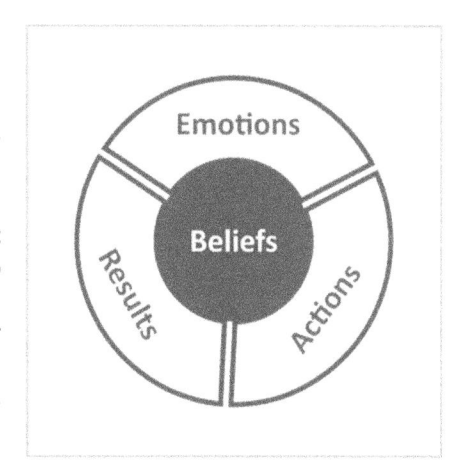

Have a professionally designed introduction and set of questions: aimed at putting the customer at ease and tested through your professional feedback systems, so they trust you as quickly as possible and you can help them make a great decision, whether it's 'yes' or 'not today', as efficiently and confidently as possible, and they enjoy and get real value from the process.

Make an 'up front contract' with the customer, that incorporates all the above, and outlines the 'win/win or no deal today' outcome.

Here's a B2B example (it's generic of course, but you'll get the picture!):

- o Our aim is to help you succeed. This is not just 'marketing waffle' but is reflected in the way we aim to do business with you. Our proposal is:
  - **To listen to you without any hidden agenda,** so we can learn about your business as deeply as possible, and what issues and opportunities have caused you to contact us. We have developed a

straightforward process for this, so you can relax and know we'll ask the most important questions that need asking, (and we'll listen to you without interrupting!). It goes without saying that everything you share with us will be treated with 100% confidentiality.

- **To only suggest products or services that will genuinely add value to you over the long and short term.** We trade on reputation above anything else, and we want you to rave about us behind our backs: we're not interested in short term sales goals, only long-term partnerships with our customers.
- **To always offer our best price.** We have transparent processes for this and we check the market every week. We don't barter or do deals to get short term custom: our aim is to build a long-term relationship of unquestioning trust between us. As you do more and more business with us, we may be able to offer better deals and more generous terms.
- **To guarantee everything we supply.** If we haven't done our job properly, it's us who should suffer, not you. On top of our standard warranties (which we believe are the best in the market), If you're not happy with anything at any time, just tell us and we'll put it right. If you're still not happy, we'll only expect you to pay what you think is right.

o In return, we ask from you:

- **To share information with us openly**, so we can genuinely find the best deals and solutions for your needs.
- To give us **continual feedback** (we'll ask!), so we can keep improving and helping you get better.
- To stick to the **agreed terms and conditions** (of course).
- And maybe occasionally to **refer a friend or colleague to us** (if we've deserved it!).

Here's a few ideas for a B2C situation (again, generic and would need to be personalised).

- **Our aim is to be truly remarkable, so that you'll buy from us again and recommend us to your friends.** To this end:
    - **Remarkable Products:** All products are presented with open reviews run by (3rd party). If they get regular bad reviews, we stop stocking them.
    - **Remarkable Service:** we're here 24/7, so you can speak to or email us at any time.
    - **Remarkable Deals:** we aim to give the best deals in our market at any time. If you find a better deal online within 48 hours, we'll refund the difference plus 20% for your trouble.
    - **Remarkable Deliveries:** all products are despatched the same day by registered post.
    - **Remarkable Attention:** we also send you (XYZ: your 'blow their socks off approach) with every order, so you can (XYZ: action).
    - **Remarkable After Sales:** we guarantee everything we sell for a full year. If you're not happy with anything, used or unused, just send it back to us and we'll refund or replace it at your discretion.
- **In return you can help us be continually remarkable by:**
    - **Giving us feedback** (we'll ask, but we are always keen to have your feedback, no matter how trivial it may seem, small things really matter!).
    - **Referring us to your friends** (if you agree that we've been remarkable). We'll send you a special deal once a month that you can take advantage of and pass on to one (and only one) good friend!
    - Happy shopping!

PLEASE NOTE:

Don't just copy 'what sounds good' in a parrot fashion, put some real thought and effort into this: take it slowly: what do your customers really value? What issues are endemic in the market? How can you stand out for the right reasons? What would be genuinely remarkable?

Make sure you mean it. Worse than making no promises would be making promises you don't mean and can't sustain (which, in the old world, was a process called 'advertising'). Customers will rightly crucify insincerity and inconsistency.

Build all these up inch by inch: it's a marathon not a sprint: don't try to 'get it all right' on day 1.

Put systems, processes and lead measures behind all your promises: you need to make sure you keep them, AND you need to make sure you keep on improving them. By the time your competitors catch up with you, you need to have innovated and moved on.

Slow Targets

Of course, everything to do with the idea of 'Slow Selling' only works as long as the targets are focused on the 'Desired activity'. Because 'what gets measured gets done'.

An Organisation will cause chaos and giant levels of stress if they state they want 'Slow Selling' but they put in place 'Fast Targets'.

This is a MASSIVE issue for many Organisations, who are often under significant stakeholder pressure for 'Fast Results' (and therefore 'Fast Targets'). But it's common sense that this type of pressure will force people in the Organisation into 'Fast Actions' in order to get 'Fast Results'. Which all too often ruins their reputation and customer relationship ... resulting in 'Slow Failure'.

And you don't need us to waste space in this book outlining examples of this happening ... it's in the news every day, and you also experience it every day in poor service delivery and frustrating actions of the unenlightened organisations who we are all too often surrounded with.

So targets need to be 'SLOW'.

What does this mean in practice? I think it's quite simple really: target the actions of 'Slow Selling', incentivise and hold people RIGOROUSLY accountable to them, and the sales results will follow (as an output). In simple terms, obsessively and rigorously identify and measure the inputs, and the outputs will take care of themselves.

What sort of 'inputs' might you measure? The answer is: anything that's outlined in the book, or anything that produces the 'Slow Selling' behaviour you're after. For example:

Service Standards

Delivery standards

Execution quality

Customer Opinion

Customer Loyalty

Of course, it would be counterproductive to just measure these, and then expect the right results to follow: you must have a balanced mix, to ensure that it's a genuine win/win: you need to be 'nice' and 'effective'.

- **'Niceness' without 'effectiveness' will put you out of business with a smile on your face.**
- **'Effectiveness' without 'niceness' will destroy loyalty and make you very vulnerable to any kind of competition.**

There is a very important place for 'traditional', results based, 'lag' measures: they still need measuring and achieving: no success is any real success without long term sensible profitability!

EMOTIONS

Slow Names

Perhaps the word 'selling' has been so misused in your Industry, and carries such negative baggage, that changing the name of your activity and department may be a great idea. If so, here are a couple of suggestions:

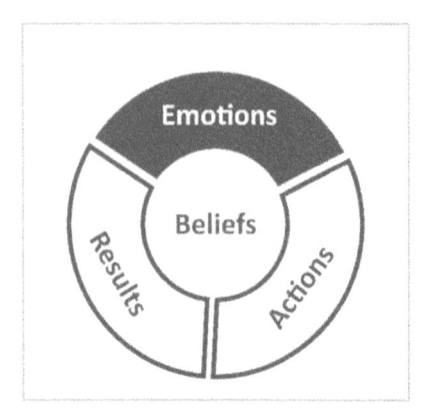

- **WAND (as in 'waving a magic ...'): which stand for**
  - **W: 'Win/win is the outcome we want, no exceptions**
  - **A: 'And the only other alternative is'**
  - **ND: 'No Deal'**
- **HEYOGEBERE (The 'Hey Yogi Bear' approach)**
  - **Our aim is to**
  - **HElpYOuGEtBEtterREsults**
  - **No exceptions**

Have fun making your own: send us your successful examples via our website and we'll share them!

Slow Listening

Ask permission to ask questions and listen first: it's good manners, and you'd want to be treated like that, wouldn't you?

Train everyone in the difficult art of 'slow listening' (see box).

Remember: in communication, slow is fast and fast is slow: you cannot be 'efficient' with people!

Customers aren't interested in how much you know until they know how much you care! One of the best ways to show attention, genuine care and build trust is to be an amazing listener.

Most people don't get enough attention in life: being a great empathic listener will make you much more influential.

Listening is a key selling tool: it takes time: do it slowly and properly and your sales will speed up.

Slow Tip:

Have fun!
Think up your own names.

'Slow Listening': 5 key Rules

1. You are here to LISTEN and UNDERSTAND from THEIR POINT OF VIEW only! Provide them with your undivided attention.

2. Be non-judgemental. Don't interrupt, advise, probe, interpret or evaluate!

3. Read the speaker. Observe the emotions behind the words. Respond to the emotion as well as the words.

4. Be Quiet. Ask open questions to clarify ONLY: nothing else. And only ask them, when the speaker has a break.

5. Assure your understanding. Reflect and restate what you perceive the speaker to be saying.

It also helps to make notes, so you can listen better, catch the important information, and deal with the issues raised (in due course) without interrupting.

Slow Tip:

There is a universal and basic human need for 'attention', and it's rarely being met adequately in today's hyper-speedy world. Being remarkable at gathering feedback, listening and showing attention is a great way to make people want to buy from you.

ACTIONS & EMOTIONS

Slow Problem Solving

Take it slowly: people won't tell you their deepest secrets in the first 5 minutes of meeting!

You need to ensure you have a wonderful, professional problem-solving process that builds relationships of uncompromising trust, in all circumstances. This does not come by chance, this comes by design.

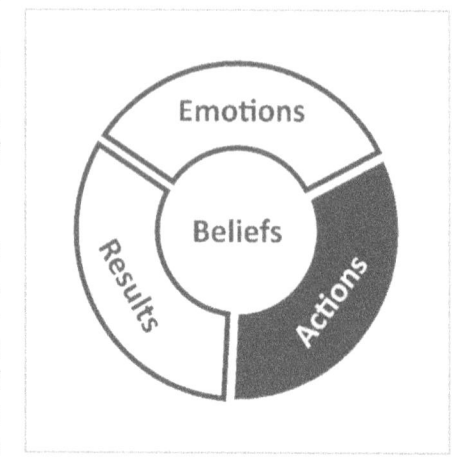

Here is what you need:

An upfront Win-win set up, promises and behaviour contract (as outlined above).

Manners that give you permission to build a relationship.

Fabulous 'Slow Listening' skills.

A professional Win-win or no deal today process that add value by building relationships, forcing you to act in a trustworthy way and adding huge value to the customer throughout. We have included one in the appendix at the end of the book, but, be very careful: this needs to be thought through very carefully from your customer's point of view, and should definitely not be copied in any way. In order to set this up properly and professionally, you need to:

Map the customer journey from initial contract to after sales.

Design every step on the way using slow selling principles.

Obsessively gather feedback from customers, and use this feedback to continually improve your processes.

The purpose of the slow problem-solving process is to help the customer find the best solution to their needs, whether they buy from you or not today. You need to see yourself as the expert in your market, helping the customer, through professional coaching, to get the best results their long-term needs. Do not obsess about getting the sale today: if you build great relationships of trust and value, the customers are much more likely to change their needs and desires to fit in with trading with you over the long term.

(And remember, if the customer is only trading on price, you are probably better off not having them as a customer, because they will be disloyal and difficult to deal with).

Slow Onion Peeling

Now you have a process, you need to operate it properly.

We call this "onion peeling": the aim is to peel away the layers (the peripheral issues and material that the customer will want to speak with you about to start with), to get to the core of the issues and find out what the real pain or opportunity is that they want solved.

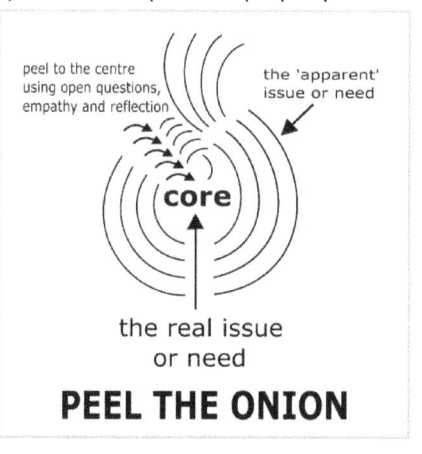

peel to the centre using open questions, empathy and reflection

the 'apparent' issue or need

core

the real issue or need

PEEL THE ONION

This is achieved by having a remarkable system (see above), and operating it remarkably with a remarkable frame of mind. This is, of course, very hard to do well, which is why you will do so brilliantly well if you manage to master it.

The key to "onion peeling" is to stick to the rules and avoid getting carried away by anything that isn't covered in this book.

Some key guidelines are as follows:

- o **Leave your ego in your car:** your customer doesn't care a damn what your sales targets are, or how much bonus you want to make this month. This is not about you: this is about the customer, and their commercial and emotional needs... Nothing else!
- o **Slow down continually,** especially when they give you a yellow light signal. By this we mean that you will pick up when a customer is less than 100% happy with the way that your discussions are going. You need to pick this up through body language, action or tone of voice, even when the customer doesn't tell you in so many words (which is usually the case!). You need to have the intelligence and strength of personality to look out for these problems, and the confidence and courage to address them when they arise. But do not be tempted to try and rush past them in the hope that they will go away: they will not go away and instead they will

> This rule is handy to remember as: **"slow down for yellow lights and turn them either red or green by peeling the onion"**
>
> In order to do this effectively you need what is called a 'three part response': it goes like this:
>
> "I'm confused, (*then state the problem*),
>
> Our aim is to find a great solution for you whether you buy from us or not today,
>
> Please help me understand you better and tell me what you think we should do".

just get worse and they will come back and bite you later on down the road.
- If this happens, you will not only have not made any sale, but you would also have ruined a relationship, and also made the whole process unnecessary stressful and costly for both of you.
- Ask open questions, and listen brilliantly.
  - Open questions are the tool of choice for great leaders and true winners. They show that you:
    - Are genuinely interested in the other person (and the other person will LOVE you for this, because it's so rare).
    - Are genuinely interested in helping them find the best solution for them, whether they buy from you today or not.
    - Are professional and want to find out the full facts.
  - They also put you at an unfair advantage in any discussion because, as long as you are also good at 'slow listening' (see above), they allow you to find out huge amounts of valuable information about the other person, and their deepest needs, which then enables you to frame what you say in terms that are important and interesting to them … and they will want to engage with you!
  - They key open words to use, to start your open questions are:
    - **Who?**
    - **What?**
    - **Where?**
    - **When?**
    - **How?**
    - **Which?**
  - These questions are fabulous tools for 'peeling the onion', and building a remarkable relationship.
- We suggest that there is one more open question, that is usually worth avoiding, and that is 'Why?'.
  - The reason for this is that this word is often used in a direct and confrontational way, and often as a

criticism. For example, when you were 5 years old and you spilt your milk, your parents might have shouted 'Why did you spill your milk!': this question was not a cue for an in-depth discussion on muscle and nerve development in a 5 year old's arm, it was a rebuke and an exclamation of frustration!
- Here's an illustration in practice:
  - A potential client tells you 'I want to achieve an uplift in XYZ'.
  - If you then ask: 'Why do you want to achieve that?' it may be OK, but it also may be too direct and confrontational, and you may receive in reply a caged answer (little or no help at all) or even a rebuke!
  - Instead, if you change the questions to: 'What are the main reasons for that?', 'How has the target been set?' or 'Which targets will that affect most?', you're far more likely to be seen as positive, helpful and collaborative, and get a reply that further builds the relationship, and, by the way, gives you valuable extra information.
- So, a simple rule: try to avoid using the question 'Why'.

o Here are a few open questions to use as 'Get out of Jail free' questions, when you don't know what question to ask next. We suggest that you note them, memorise them, and use them whenever you feel stuck … you'll be amazed at how helpful they are!
- When you're talking about a 'problem' that the customer has:
  - 'And then what happens?'
- When you're talking about an 'opportunity' a customer has:
  - 'What might that enable you to do that you can't do now?'
- When you want to know more:
  - 'What examples do you have of that?'
- And when you're lost or confused:

- 'I'm confused, what do you really mean by that?'
- Or: 'I don't fully understand that: what do I need to know in order to understand it better?'
- Make notes
  - Come on! You can't remember everything: if you don't take notes your customer may think you're arrogant or uninterested. And your ability to do slow listening and onion peeling will be severely curtailed.
  - If you do, and you do it properly, you'll come across as seriously interested, organised, professional and collaborative. Done properly, it will give you the calmness, objectivity and organisation you need, not only to do some great 'slow listening' but also some great 'onion peeling'.
  - We suggest you produce yourself a 'sales process guide sheet' using the 'win/win agreement format' (see Appendix below), personalised for the issues and circumstances that are peculiar to your industry and customer needs. We have produced these for countless clients and many different Industries: they usually share 80% of the 'standard' guidelines (as outlined in the Appendix) but need 20% personalisation to meet specific needs.
- Discriminate between problems and opportunities
  - As briefly mentioned above: it's very important at all times to keep an objective focus on where you are in the conversation, and, in particular, whether your customer is talking about a 'problem' or an 'opportunity'.
  - Why is this important: 3 reasons:
    - Firstly: when they are talking about 'problems' they may be stressed and worried: so it's vital for you to be calm, slow and empathic. They are usually 3 or 4 times as ready to 'buy' when in this emotional

state, but it's VITAL that you don't take advantage of this in any way, either consciously or sub consciously. (If you do, as soon as they calm down, they'll realise this and NEVER trust you again). This is where they'll REALLY thank you for slowing them down, coaching and helping them, building the relationship and peeling the onion. This is where you can build life-long relationships of mutual trust and value.

- Secondly: when they're talking about 'opportunities' they're likely to be over optimistic with themselves and with any budget they may need. It's MUCH harder for them to get funding for opportunities than it is for solving problems. The reason is that 'problems' are factual and easy to measure and justify, whereas 'opportunities' are subjective, open to different opinions, and hard to measure. So, your job is to slow down, slow them down, use your systems, peel the onion, look for key measurables, focus on them and how hard they will find it to justify any action or expense. Work collaboratively with them and synergistically work up a win/win plan that's sensible and as factual as possible. By doing this, you may not get that sale today, but you will get life-long client loyalty, and massive sales in the future. Very often in this case:
- If you go for the 'quick sale' it comes back to bite you with complaints and poor reputation: a massive lose/lose.
- If you go for the 'slow sale', the customer may change their plans and specs to include your product or service over the long term: a massive win/win.
- Thirdly: the open questions you use should be different depending on the circumstances you're in (see guidance above).

Slow Tip

Use '4 colour pens' – remember those pens you used to have at school? It turns out that they are much more useful that that expensive pen you were given for your birthday. The reason is that, with a '4 colour pen' you can:

Make mind maps

Insert coloured reminders, so you don't have to interrupt your customer (which kills the relationship … VERY important)

Insert thoughts and ideas you have while you're listening, and distinguish them easily form your 'standard' notes

Write different categories of notes in different colours. For information only, we use:

>Black for facts

>Blue for information

>Red for issues

>Green for ideas or agreed actions

The better tools you have, and the greater your attention to detail, the easier you'll find it to stick to the point, focus on 'Slow Selling' and get more and better customers.

Slow Value Creation

The key in any sales relationship is to establish the REAL VALUE to the customer: you do this SLOWLY: the customer is often not aware of the real needs and certainly often shy and unwilling to open up to 'sales people'.

On top of this, they are continually bombarded by old fashioned 'sales shouting' of 'special offers' and 'never to be repeated deals'.

In a nutshell, they are often, confused, misled and rightfully wary.

Your job is to be a slow professional and earn their trust and loyalty, slowly, step by step, to help them understand the real need they have and the real value you can bring.

Your product or service has NO VALUE unless it solves REAL problems for the customer. It doesn't matter how flashy or well wrapped up it may be: if you have integrity, the only thing you want to be listening and talking about is the customer, their real needs and, eventually, as an outcome of doing the above brilliantly, you may be allowed to demonstrate how your product or service adds value and solves these needs … properly.

Slow Pricing

Price!

How embarrassing people often find it to talk sensibly about price!

Customers lie about their price aspirations, and sellers lie about the true value of their product.

In the absence of great thinking, great processes and great systems, 'speedy sellers' can often end up in a price-cutting race to the bottom.

SLOW SELLERS DON'T DO THIS.

Slow Sellers are up front, open and straight about their price: this is because they're professionals with integrity: they have quality systems that build value for the customer at every step, they know the market, they charge fair prices, they offer guarantees and they continually blow the customers' socks off.

In B2C situations they will usually also offer a price comparison guarantee (and they will be up front and proactive with it), as this is vital for customer trust. They will also give a customer promise that loyal customers will always have the same or a better deal than new customers.

In B2B situations, they'll know their place in the market, why they're more expensive than some, and why they're less expensive than others. They'll be proud of the VALUE they deliver for the price they charge, they'll be open and up front, they will always quote the best rate they can for the situation first time, they'll offer a best rate guarantee, they won't haggle under pressure (as this just proves they're untrustworthy), they'll offer additional discounts with volume, and they will always make sure their existing customers benefit first (before new customers) with any special deals,

One of the best tools that a professional Slow Seller can use when dealing with B2B or large B2C purchases, is to 'test the range' during the win/win process. They do this by bringing up price early (preferably before the customer does), and doing the following:

Peeling the onion to find out the key real needs.

Reflecting these back.

Then being up front by 'testing the range': they say something like: 'People/organisations wanting (ABC service / these kind of results) typically invest/spend between X and Y: how does that range sound to you?'

Then they can determine the next steps by the answer:

- **Range OK:** proceed as instructed here.
- **Range too high:** what are their real expectations? Have you understood them right? Are they being realistic? Do they have enough of an issue or opportunity to justify the spend? Time for lots of great onion peeling and open questions to turn this 'yellow light' either red or green for all the right reasons.
- **Range too low:** Have you understood the full scope of their needs? Is your solution high enough quality for them? Are they expecting more of you than you anticipate? Time for lots of great onion peeling and open questions to turn this 'yellow light' either red or green for all the right reasons.

Slow Alternatives

Professional Slow Sellers take the time to investigate all the alternatives for and with the customer: even if you can't meet all of them. The aim is to help the customer get the best results, remember, whether they buy from you today or not! You're the expert in your field, and your customer needs you to help them, genuinely and holistically: do this remarkably, and they are much more likely to buy from you, come back to you and rave about you to their friends … even if your alternative wasn't necessarily the best on paper …

RESULTS

Slow Facts and Measures

The most important things you're looking for, by professionally executing this slow selling process, are the key facts and measures. This is because facts and measures:

- Help you understand the customer better.
- Help the customer clarify the situation in their own mind.
- Ensure that any potential solution can be stress tested against the facts, to see how it stacks up.

These facts and measures can take time to find: that's OK, you're slow selling!

The best way to get these vital facts and measures out on the table is by peeling the onion, asking open questions, and then using specific questions when you hear something that might be measurable. Here are the specific questions (Note: they are all 'open' questions!):

For 'problems':

- And then what happens?
- How do you measure that?
- How large is the problem?
- What does this cost (directly and indirectly)?
- How long might this go on for (if not solved)?
- How much might you be prepared to spend/invest to sort this out?

For 'opportunities':

- What would that enable you to do that you can't do at the moment?
- How might you measure that?
- What's the current figure?
- What would you want it to be?
- What's the value of the difference?
- Over how long?

Let them do all the maths and hard work: I know this sounds odd when you're trying to build a remarkable relationship, but this is vital for the following reasons:

o These have to be their figures, not yours.
o They often haven't thought it through properly before you asked, and they need to in order to make the best decision for them.

Just for info: here are a few examples of statements that a customer might make that would indicate that there may be some facts and measures you need to clarify here:
- B2B
    - We need our sales team to be more effective.
    - We need to get more out of our advertising.
    - We need to increase customer spend.
    - We want to develop our XYZ.
    - We need to be more productive.
- B2C
    - We struggle with …
    - We want to change …
    - We want more of …
    - We want less of …

Slow Outcomes

So, by now, if you've done all the above properly, you should be approaching some 'outcomes'. Remember, **the outcomes the customer wants will vary, but their emotional need for, trust, attention and an easier life will never change**: so our outcome is to ensure we do a remarkable job, whatever happens.

Remember
- A sale today for the right reasons is a short and long-term win/win.
- A 'no sale' today for the right reasons is a long-term win/win.
- A sale today for the wrong reasons is a short-term win/lose and a long term lose/lose.
- A 'no sale' today for the wrong reasons is a short term lose/win and a long term lose/lose.

How to get to a slow outcome: the process

- Use the slow selling win/win process.
- Build the relationship.
- When you are getting near the end of the process, start to indicate that this is your opinion and you're looking to bring this to one of the first 2 outcomes above: say something like:
    - It looks like we've discussed everything in full, is it OK to check with you what I understand?
- Precis your understanding and reflect it back to them.
- Keep alert for additions (then add them in to the process using the win/win tool, then go back to getting to a slow outcome), and reflect back again.
- Ask them if that's right. Keep alert for more additions (then add them in to the process also using the win/win tool, and go back to getting to a slow outcome).
- Repeat until they can genuinely say: 'Yes, that's exactly right'.
- Then go for the outcome:
    - Remind them of the win/win up front agreement: ask them for one of three answers today:
        - Definitely yes.
        - Definitely no.
        - I need time to think about it / do some more research and I'd like to talk with you again on an agreed date.
    - If you're convinced you can help them today with 100% integrity, outline your proposed solution (paying particular attention to the facts and measures and how you can solve these).
    - If you're not 100% sure, tell them so, outline what you think would be the best solution today, but tell them you want to do some more thinking/research and you'd like to make an appointment to get back to them on an agreed date and time.

Slow Guarantees

Slow Sellers offer guarantees and are very up front about them. This not only builds customer trust quickly, but also gives them a continual impetus to ensure they are always performing to their top standard.

Guarantees are just blindingly obvious common sense: if your customer wasn't happy for any reason, you'd want them to tell you first and give you the opportunity of putting it right (before they ruin your reputation online), wouldn't you?

Guarantees also give you valuable feedback to help you learn and grow: our own 'no quibble guarantee' has been invoked on three occasions in all the time we've been coaching and training:

- o On two occasions the customer was right: we learnt hugely valuable lessons and also developed a stronger a better relationship with them.
- o On one occasion, we considered the customer was being unreasonable and we learnt that we had a customer we needed to stop working with!

People often ask us: 'Don't people take advantage of a guarantee': well, in the grand scope of life, perhaps 1% of people will do this: the real issue is not to worry about the 1% (you can NEVER please everyone: they are a cost of being remarkable ... and even they sometimes have valuable lessons for you). The key is to focus on the 99% where you have truly delivered a remarkable experience, and with whom you have slowly built an army of loyal customers, and passionate referrers.

Make sure your guarantees are as simple, honest and unequivocal as possible: this is not a time to let the marketing, legal or PR dept push you into mealy mouthed mush:

- o B2C Guarantees include:
    - Price match guarantees

- Product happiness guarantees
- Delivery guarantees
- Service guarantees
 - B2B Guarantees include:
    - Best rate guarantees
    - Happiness guarantees
    - Transparency guarantees
    - Product or service update guarantees
    - Renewal price guarantees (this is a big one: Insurance Companies please note!)
    - You get offers before new customers guarantees

EMOTIONS, RESULTS & ACTIONS

Slow Follow-Ups

This is one of the few areas where it's good to be faster than usual!

Go out of your way to follow up your sale (or 'no sale today') and do it genuinely: with the aim of building the relationship further and cementing your customer loyalty.

This can be anything from:

- Proactive and service delivery updates.
- Proactive check backs.
- Proactive sending of extra information or welcome packs.

Your business is unique: you need to build your follow-ups slowly and methodically using customer feedback.

We remember a friend who is also a builder joking with us about his guarantee: 'We offer a tail light guarantee on all our work: for as long as you can see my tail lights, it's guaranteed'. The key on follow ups is to have exactly the opposite mindset to this!

Slow Feedback

And lastly: all sales need proactive slow feedback.

Feedback is the breakfast of champions: gather it obsessively and proactively and use it to continually improve and further deliver a remarkable experience and build great relationships.

But you need to be slower than the norm: most feedback today is done by email and online 'web surveys':

- Are these enjoyable for your customer? No
- Are these in any way remarkable? No
- Do these build a relationship and add value? No
- Do these allow the customer to tell you what they REALLY think? No

In other words, most feedback systems being used today are a monumental waste of time that ruin your customer relationship!

Your feedback system needs to be right for your type of customer interaction:

- For 'transactional' (selling basic stuff) interactions you need a very short and simple online score and one question feedback operation.
- For 'emotional' (selling higher value stuff, and higher value discretionary spend) interactions, you need a very short and simple phone feedback (with prior warning and agreed participation).
- For 'relationship' (all B2B and all professional, long term B2C business) interactions you need high quality phone (or even face to face) feedback, using a professional 3rd party, (with prior warning and agreed participation).

Relationship	in depth professional 3rd party
Emotional	short open by phone
Transactional	short & simple automated

DIFFERENT FEEDBACK APPROACHES FOR DIFFERENT BUYING RELATIONSHIP

Professional Feedback Systems: Key Rules

1. HONESTY OF DATA

The customer just wants to tell you what they think, honestly ... without embarrassment or upset. You need to ensure the feedback system uses open questions and allows the customer to tell you about what's important to them (not for you to ask about what's important to you).

2. PROVIDES PERSPECTIVE

This needs to be a system that provides clear perspective: it's not a tool to judge, scold or should about: it's a perspective tool to help you do the right thing continually, inch by inch.

3. PERMISSION BASED & HOLISTIC

As explained above: it must be permission-based for the customer and a holistic part of the whole way you do business: otherwise it's just an 'add-on' that can be conveniently ignored. Holistic also means that you treat your 'internal customers' in the same way and continually listen to them and value their feedback.

4. 'LISTENING FEEDBACK' NOT A 'SURVEY'

Remember, customers just want to be valued and listened to: do not confuse feedback with a survey: this is not a set of questions you want the answer to, this is a powerful and obsessive system to genuinely understand the voice of the customer.

5. HIGH RESPONSE RATES

Judge the success of the feedback system by the response rates and how many times the customer says 'thanks for asking'. Keep tweaking it inch by inch to improve these numbers.

Slow loyalty

> ### 6. HIGH VALUE WITH A 'LEAD MEASURE' THAT PEOPLE KNOW
> You'll know this is working well when your people are focused on it and look forward to getting more of it. They will also know the measure and be focused on improving it in their role.
>
> ### 7. PEACE OF MIND
> You'll know when the 'system is working' when you feel peace of mind that you've got your finger on the pulse and that effective direct and indirect response systems are driving your business forward.

And the last piece in the jigsaw is to add in:
- Customer Loyalty.
- Up sales and cross sales.

Again, the key is to take it slowly: the whole point of slow selling, apart from being more professional and having a better system so you get the best outcome for both of you, is to build long term relationships of mutual trust and mutual benefit because you've been remarkable. And this, in financial terms, means:

- Quicker and larger repeat sales.
- Easy cross and up sales.
- Increased direct and indirect referrals.

Lets' examine the philosophy here first, then look at each of these areas briefly in turn (even though you could strictly argue that these do not fit in to the idea of 'slow selling' as they rarely involve much sales effort (because you've already paid the price to build the remarkable relationship), nor are they usually 'slow' (as customers with whom you have a remarkable relationship are usually quick and keen to buy more, buy bigger, buy other things and rave about you to their friends and online). This is very different from the 'traditional' approach to selling (where the first sale is done as fast as possible, and thus usually results in any subsequent sales being slow and hard).

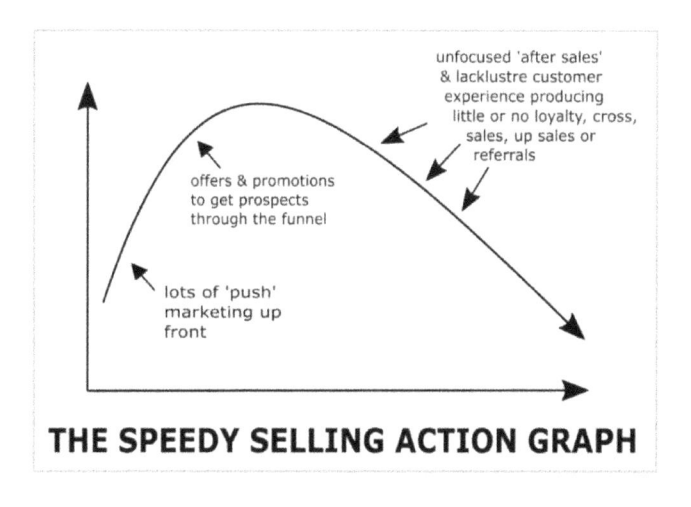

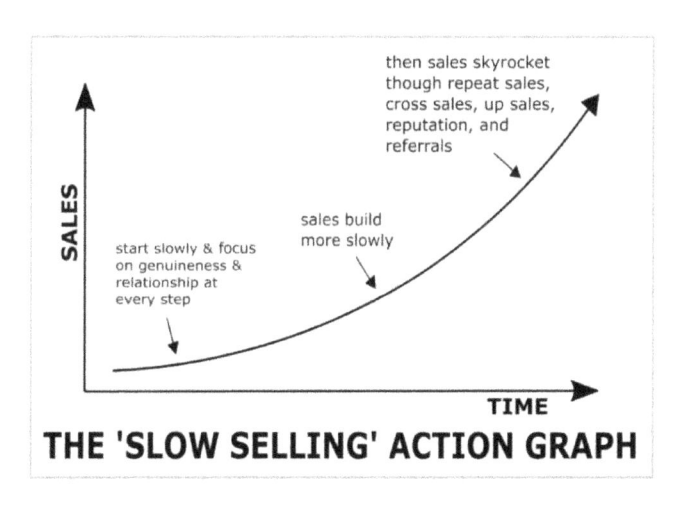

THE SPEEDY SELLING ACTION GRAPH

Labels on graph:
- lots of 'push' marketing up front
- offers & promotions to get prospects through the funnel
- unfocused 'after sales' & lacklustre customer experience producing little or no loyalty, cross, sales, up sales or referrals

THE 'SLOW SELLING' ACTION GRAPH

Axes: SALES (vertical), TIME (horizontal)

Labels on graph:
- start slowly & focus on genuineness & relationship at every step
- sales build more slowly
- then sales skyrocket though repeat sales, cross sales, up sales, reputation, and referrals

Starting point: you can only get mountains of repeat sales, cross sales, up sales and referrals, if you get the slow selling process right first: no exceptions.

- So we assume that you've done everything as instructed above, so far: you now have remarkable customer relationships, and some solid and profitable sales coming in: you now need to leverage the relationships, slowly, to build repeat sales, cross sales and referrals.

Also: **CUSTOMER LOYALTY IS NOT FREE**: you have to invest in it continually and obsessively (just as you do in your marketing to find new customers). But it is significantly more profitable per $ spent than any spend on 'traditional' marketing: between 6 and 20 times more profitable. DO NOT LET YOUR FINANCE PEOPLE MAKE YOU CUT BACK IN THIS AREA SIMPLY BECAUSE THEY CANT IMMEDIATELY MEASURE THE OUTPUT OF DOING THIS RIGHT: because if you're not up front and obsessive with this, that's exactly what they'll do ... then all your hard work in 'slow selling' will go out of the window, and eventually you'll give up and go back to the bad old 'fast selling' processes. This is absolutely vital!

The process now is:

- **Keep building the relationship above all else:** the customer should want to be loyal to you, buy more, review you online and rave about you to their friends, but you need to take it slowly, and NEVER abuse the relationship by considering and acting on your priorities above theirs: their loyalty has taken a lot of time and effort to earn ... it will only take one thoughtless act or inappropriate communication to blow it forever. This is a complicated and delicate area, but very worth it.

Make sure all you do is:

- ✓ **Guided by your 'Customer Focused Mission'** (this is your compass).
- ✓ **Filtered through the 'Customers' REAL Needs'** of **Trust**, Attention, and an easier Life (this is your filter).

- ✓ **Introduced and acted upon in small steps** – 'Go the Extra Inch' – so you learn slowly what works, what's appropriate and what isn't (this is your action instruction).
- ✓ **Is measured and monitored by continual professional feedback processes**, that also act as relationship and loyalty builders in their execution – this is a hard and specialised area to get right: be very cautious (this is also your check and balance and your information generator to help you continually improve, innovate and know what steps to take next, both individually and systemically).

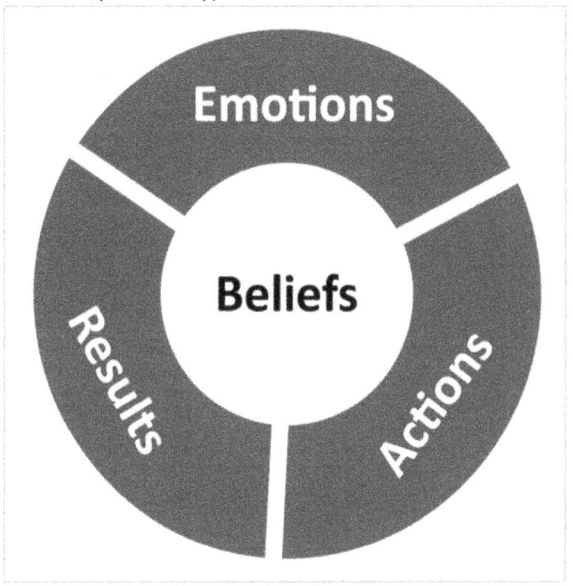

Emotions / Beliefs / Results / Actions

If you do all the above properly, you'll slowly learn, and be guided by the best consultant in your business (the customer) on what to start, stop and continue doing to build repeat sales, up sales cross sales and referrals.

This information will be more relevant and valuable than anything we can write in the next page or so, so please read and understand some of the ideas we'll put forward below, but always listen to your customers (internal and external) first, and filter everything through what you hear.

Slow repeat sales, up sales & cross sales

Some suggestions of what you can proactively do to build repeat sales, up sales, cross sales and referrals might be:

- Repeat sales
  - GATHER CONTINUAL PROFESSIONAL FEEDBACK FIRST.
  - Create loyalty clubs and systems that add genuine value (and are not a marketing triumph of appearance over content as can so often be the case).
  - Special offers that are unique to loyal customers (and not available to anyone else).
  - Keeping loyal customers informed about special offers up front (that you are advertising to attract new customers).
  - Be up front and say that you want their loyalty and what systems and ideas you'll be communicating in order to EARN this.
  - Continual small actions, from your feedback to continually raise the game, improve their experience and blow their socks off: Go the Extra Inch! (Note: they'll only notice these subconsciously as you do them, but they'll notice very consciously and vocally if you don't!!). Don't expect miracles: customer loyalty is a continual slow process of sticking to your beliefs and to the ideas and principles set out in this book.
  - The small actions you now take with loyal customers will add HUGE value to the relationship and will pay you back in spades. DON'T BE STINGY … EVER! No one wants to be loyal to a stingy person or Organisation. Some examples of getting it right:
  - A food supplier adding in a couple of free lemons when a customer buys a fresh chicken.
  - Offering a free half day's coaching / training for a successful candidate when completing a recruitment process for a client.

- Genuinely carefully selected partner offers that add extra value to loyalty systems.

o Up sales
  - Make sure any 'up sales' processes comply with your 'Customer Focused Mission'. Remember: you're here

> **Always remember your internal customer: your people**
>
> This whole book has been focused on 'selling' to your external customer. But, in the same way, you also need to continually 'sell' to your internal customer (to build relationships and remarkable loyalty from them), and more importantly, you need to obsessive get feedback from them, listen to them and use their views as the best consultancy information you can ever get.
>
> The reason for this is that not only do they care more than everyone else (as they have more at stake), but also they will be more critical of your systems and processes as they can see them in their entirety, warts and all.

  to do remarkable things so that sales will follow, not the other way around.
  - Learn what products naturally 'offer more value in higher quantities' in the mind of the customer: what are their 'real needs', from your continual professional feedback. How can you make their life easier by buying more or bigger now, rather than waiting until later?

- Take it slowly: don't let your sales and marketing people loose on this! Develop your up sales systems in small steps. What processes will add value and make you more remarkable and what instead might sell more in the short term but will detract from your remarkability in the long?
- When you have a great deal, put a limit on it, so that many customers have the opportunity to benefit from it (and not just a few customers who buy in bulk).
- Create 'long term buying up' systems that reward customers over the long term for loyalty and extra sales.
- Use your feedback systems to measure effectiveness and customer interpretation of your processes.
- Think outside the box (using your feedback to supercharge this): what remarkable things could you do that will result in both you selling more today and leaving the customer wowed?

o Cross sales
  - Make sure any 'cross sales' processes comply with your 'Customer Focused Mission'. Remember: you're here to do remarkable things so that sales will follow, not the other way around.
  - Be very careful: cross selling can tempt you very quickly to compromise your principles in a quest for quick and easy short-term profits. Done wrong, they can destroy your customer relationship in an instant … done right they can supercharge your bottom line while also building fantastic levels of reputation and loyalty!
  - Learn what products naturally 'go together' in the mind of the customer. How can you make their life easier by offering packages for them? How can you show that you're listening by altering and tweaking these packages to make them ever more attractive to the customer? How can you ensure that these packages are packaged and priced in a way that

builds uncompromising trust in the quality and value of the packages?
- Develop cross sales systems slowly in small steps to ensure you're adding value and building relationships (and not the opposite!).
- Use your feedback systems to measure effectiveness and customer interpretation.
- Think outside the box (using your feedback to supercharge this): what remarkable things could you do, and what amazing partnerships can you create that will result in you cross selling amazingly and leaving the customer wowed?

Slow Referrals

Direct and Indirect referrals will naturally come from doing the 'Slow Selling' processes remarkably, holistically and synergistically, but you need to make it easy for the customer to help you (after all, they're busy and have got many other things on their mind). Here are a few KEY things you might do:

- Know who your target customers are and have a clear description of them that your existing customer can easily understand.
- Know what key problems you solve ideally for customers.
- Talk about the above two items in all your literature and put in hints in suitable places about how you prefer to spend your money 'making sure your customers get the best deals and the best backup rather than on advertising' so you're 'always happy to receive referrals' and 'always treat referrals like gold dust' (and that you won't let them down if they refer you).
- Be fun, upbeat and remarkable in the way you do all this.

- Put easy to follow steps in place that make it really easy for people to refer you: leaflets, links, events, ideas etc etc (that are valuable in themselves and are attractive and easy for your customer to give to others).

Here's an example of how you'd add a 'direct referral process' into a telephone feedback process:
- When you've asked your key questions, listened and peeled the onion properly, ask
  - Is it OK to ask 2 specific questions?
  - If 'yes' go forward, if 'no' thank them for their time and input
- B2C:
  - If you had to rate the experience out of 10, what would the score be?
    - 0-6: that doesn't sound like the sort of experience they'd want you to have: can we ask them to call you asap to sort it out?
    - 7 or 8: that sounds like they've done ok, but not 'amazing': what would you like them to do to move that to a 9 or 10?
    - 9 or 10: that sounds like they've done the sort of job they're aiming to do: they offer a generous customer referral scheme, would you like them to send you the information, so you can pass it on to your friends?
- B2B:
  - If you had to rate the experience out of 10, what would the score be?
    - 0-6: that doesn't sound like the sort of relationship they'd want to have with you: can we ask them to call you asap to sort it out?
    - 7 or 8: that sounds like they're doing ok, but not 'amazing': what would you like them to do to move that to a 9 or 10?
    - 9 or 10: that sounds like they've done the sort of job they're aiming to do: they grow mainly through direct referrals, they don't advertise for new customers as they prefer to spend their advertising budget on delivering value and backup service to you. If they contacted you to ask, would you be willing and able to refer them to someone suitable that you know?

Part 8:
Action Plan

> 'No farmer ever ploughed his field by turning it over in his mind'
>
> Chinese Proverb

Now you've got to the end of the book, you perhaps need to do two things:

1. **Congratulate yourself**: most people never get this far in any 'self-improvement' book
2. **Make an action plan.**

Here are a few basic points to help you start an action plan and get these ideas moving in your Organisation, Team, or just by yourself. Remember: *'An ounce of actions is worth more than a ton of theory'.*

1. **Go the extra inch**
   a. Take a small action this week.
   b. Repeat weekly.
   c. Evolution NOT revolution: take it slowly.
   d. To sell these ideas to others, explain and ask … don't tell.
   e. Use the 'Go the extra inch' process.
2. **Obsessively and professionally gather feedback**
   a. This is a vital investment in customer engagement, loyalty, reputation and referrals: invest serious time and money in this, don't use a generic off the shelf cheap compromise.
   b. Do it continually and obsessively
   c. Have a professional response system for all types of feedback: 'Great' 'OK' and 'Poor'.
   d. Have your systems and feedback independently audited and accredited to make sure they are working as they should and to give the customer confidence that you're doing this properly (see Investors in Feedback:
   www.investorsinfeedback.com).

3. **Focus on building value through relationships … whether they buy or not**
   a. This should become your mantra (or what we'd probably call your 'customer focused mission').
   b. Only then will the profits follow, through loyalty, reputation, cross buying, up buying and referrals.
   c. Then put a world class referral system in place .
4. **Remember there is often a short-term price to pay: loyalty, reputation and referrals aren't free**
   a. Repeat: Slow Selling is a vital investment in customer engagement, loyalty, reputation and referrals as an end in itself, in the sure belief that, if you do this properly, the sales will follow. Invest serious time and money in this, don't panic, employ short term 'sales tactics' or use any cheap compromises.
   b. Slow Selling is a marketing expense that if effective, measurable, empowering, motivating and drives continual improvement and innovation on top. If you can see anything better to invest in, please let us know!
5. **Get outside help**
   a. Paid: coach trainer: focused on and licensed in slow selling.
   b. Unpaid: obsessive internal and external customer and non-customer feedback.
6. **Systemise for consistency and continual improvement**
   a. Systemise inch by inch, guided by the 'customer focused mission', and filtered through the 'customers' REAL needs'.
   b. Use the 'Slow Sales Process' guidance above as a template and personalise it to suit your needs and situation. Flesh it out step by step, little by little, by combining your customer feedback with the ideas put forward above.
   c. Once the steps have been discovered and agreed, start to systemise them one by one. Take it slowly and do it well. The speed will come from getting it right in slow and small steps!
7. **Start again**
   a. This is a continual process.

b. The better you get, the more vulnerable you are to complacency and the harder your competitors will try to lure your customers from you.

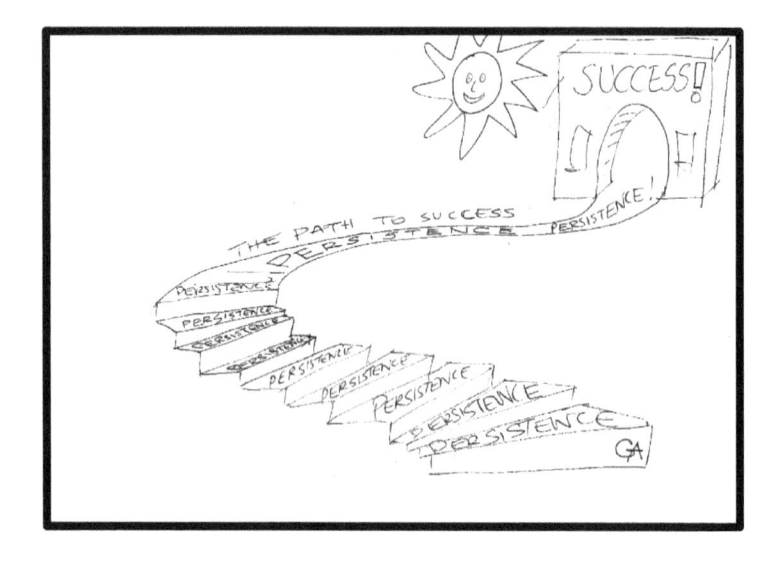

Appendix 1:
Win/win agreements

Intent	- What's the REAL win we're after? For you first, then me. - How does this conversation fit with our and your goals, targets and mission? - How should we act in order to get the best out of this process, whether we do business together or not (and either is OK)?
Desired Results	- What are the measurable results we're looking for from this activity? - Personal and organisational - Physical and emotional - THEIR WINS FIRST
Guidelines	- Agree the intent and DR and then ask them their opinions - Open questions and peel the onion - Lists, reflection and prioritisation - Have notes, questions and FACTS about what YOU think needs to be discussed - Only put your opinions forward when you get the green light
Resources	- What resources do you both need to make this happen? - If you / they don't have them, who does and how will we get them? - Time, money, people, other
Accountability	- Agree measures - Agree service quality measures and guarantees - Agree review - Agree next steps
Consequences	- Agree the consequences of success and failure - These consequences will be in 2 categories: 'natural' and 'social'

For detailed explanation, support and training on 'win/win agreements' please have a look at the 'Slow Sellers Association': www.slow-sellers.org

Appendix 2:
Sample completed win/win agreement

This is a sample outline plan to explain and guide people on a proposed coaching and support package for a client, to be used as an example to help you with your win/win agreements

Intent

a coaching and support process that adds value, is enjoyable, and is enthusiastically looked forward to each month by the team, and continually helps them develop and excel at their 'Customer Focused Mission' to **Always Care about Getting it Right**

Desired Results

- A monthly programme of short 1:1 sessions that are enthusiastically supported by all
- Resulting in at least one small step per person per session that they are committed to achieving
- That helps the individual and their team continually develop and improve and work consistently towards the execution of the Mission
- That measurably affects results and supports the achievement of the agreed goals of X, Y and Z of the business

Guidelines

The issues you have currently are

- List of issues and impacts
- How this affects the bottom line
- Upside of getting this right

(Note: there may be a lot of information here: this will all come from the guided discussions you have during the SLOW 'WOND process' as detailed above)

We have agreed to help you address these issues and achieve the desired results through

- A monthly 1:1 session for 45 minutes with each person each month.

Each session will follow this format

1. Review of last month's agreed action and output from it
2. Thoughts of problems and / or opportunities that have arisen in the last month (related or unrelated to last month's subject)
3. Discussion and coaching, centred on the Mission, about what could be done to move forward effectively
4. Agreement on the 'Extra Inch' this month (one thing to move this forward in a small way that you feel enthusiastic, committed and empowered to do), and how this will be accountable next month

Verbal briefing shared by ABC with XYZ following completion of the exercise each month (leaving out anything confidential or uncomfortable) on the key inches agreed.

XYZ to share same with the team.

(Anything that's uncomfortable or confidential discussed in the sessions will be left out of the review process and instead reviewed confidentially with the individual in a way that they agree to beforehand: we are professionally obliged (and personally committed) to maintain any confidentialities at all times).

Resources

Resources that will help with this process are:

General
- Agreed resources at the meeting (eg YouTube video on a specific point discussed)

- These specific learning points and issues address [followed by a list]
- Actions and exercises agreed to continually extend people's comfort zone
- Feedback from customers
- Feedback between your people (we need to proactively ask for and welcome feedback)
- Help each other: a problem shared is a problem halved: you are a team aiming to deliver your 'Customer Focused Mission': use this constantly and always look for ways to ask for and give help to each other
- ABC available by email or phone between sessions for ad hoc information

Time:
- Monthly full day sessions in [location]

People
- Led by XYZ
- Delivered by ABC
- Supported by all of you between you

Money
- As a long-term customer, you get 15% discount on our standard rates which are …
- This means the monthly budget is …
- Plus anticipated monthly expenses of …

Other
- This may well lead on to other activity and support (eg training, owner feedback exercise, etc etc)

Accountability

All expenditure of time, money and effort should be accountable: we offer a guarantee on all we do: if you're not happy at any stage for any reason, please tell us and we'll put it right; if you're still not happy, we only expect you to pay what you think we're worth to you.

The key measures of accountability will be:

Lead measures
- People's commitment to the extra inch each month
- People's action during the month to deliver the extra inch
- Feedback to XYZ

Lag measures
- People's action during the month to deliver the extra inch
- Measurable monthly progress on results

Consequences

- All top performers have coaches: if you are to genuinely deliver on your intent to live by the Mission, it makes sense to have a small amount of outside help to support and help you. If you do this you will have more of a chance of excelling.
- If this happens we will continue to work together to find ways to increase and improve our support and your results
- Without a coach it is far too easy to get caught in the 'rut of the mundane': if you do this, you'll definitely struggle to deliver on your mission and your budgeted results
- If the coaching is done badly, this will be a waste of time and resources. The accountability needs to be rigorously assessed every month to ensure this is delivering the value we need it to. If not, then the guarantee would be invoked and if this happens more than once this work will need to be re-examined, redefined or ceased.

Appendix 3:
Action sheet for inch by inch improvement

'Speedy Selling' process we want to change	
How does our 'Customer Focused Mission' apply to this process?	
What are our customers' emotional needs?	
Inch by inch steps we could take	
How to measure progress	
When to next review this	

This sheet and diagram can be downloaded at www.slow-selling.org

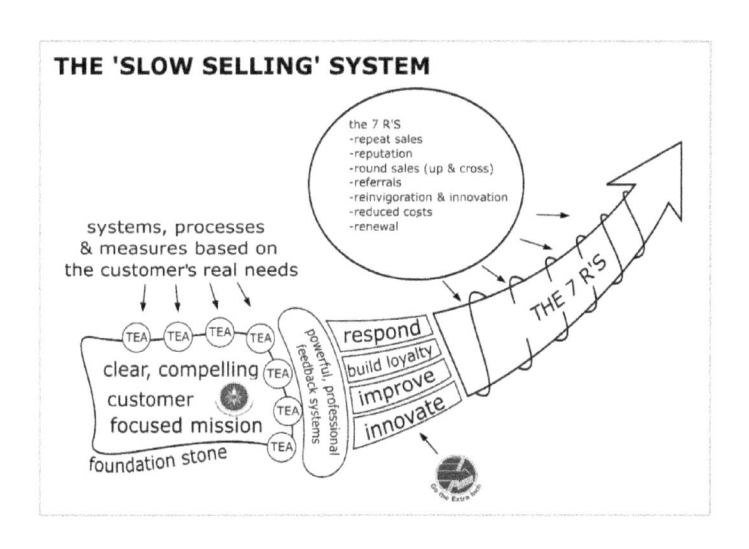

THE 'SLOW SELLING' SYSTEM

the 7 R'S
- repeat sales
- reputation
- round sales (up & cross)
- referrals
- reinvigoration & innovation
- reduced costs
- renewal

systems, processes & measures based on the customer's real needs

THE 7 R'S

clear, compelling customer focused mission

foundation stone

powerful, professional feedback systems

respond
build loyalty
improve
innovate

Appendix 4:
The 'Slow Sellers Oath'

The Slow Seller's Oath

When training to become a medical practitioner in any field, every student is asked to swear the Hippocratic Oath. Here are the key principles:

- I will apply, for the benefit of the sick, all measures that are required, avoiding those twin traps of overtreatment and therapeutic nihilism.

- I will remember that there is art to medicine as well as science, and that warmth, sympathy, and understanding may outweigh the surgeon's knife or the chemist's drug.

- I will not be ashamed to say "I know not," nor will I fail to call in my colleagues when the skills of another are needed for a patient's recovery.

- I will remember that I do not treat a fever chart, a cancerous growth, but a sick human being, whose illness may affect the person's family and economic stability. My responsibility includes these related problems, if I am to care adequately for the sick.

- I will remember that I remain a member of society, with special obligations to all my fellow human beings, those sound of mind and body as well as the infirm.

- May I always act so as to preserve the finest traditions of my calling and may I long experience the joy of healing those who seek my help.

It's common sense of course, but vitally important. It entreats the Medical Practitioner to 'rise to a higher level' and act with integrity and good faith in all matters.

In making a public declaration, they are making a strong statement to themselves and to the world that they espouse these values and are prepared to be held accountable to them. That's why it's such a strong tradition.

Because Doctors are in powerful positions of trust and influence, it's vital that there's a 'universal principle' to guide their behaviour and bind their actions.

Hence the need for the Hippocratic Oath.

We suggest that the same is true in the 'sales' process.

In this hyper-connected, customer empowered and transparent world, the reputation and trust of the individual and organisation is of paramount importance for it to thrive … and for customers to truly benefit.

We invite anyone selling anything in any profession, in order to be called a 'professional', to swear 'The Slow Sellers Oath' and be proud to stick to it. Indeed, it is a main ingredient of membership of the 'Slow Sellers Association'.

Here it is:

The Slow Seller's Oath

- I will apply, for the benefit of the customer, all measures that are required, avoiding those twin traps of overpromising and under delivery.

- I will remember that there is art to business as well as science, and that warmth, empathy, and trustworthiness will outweigh any sales or marketing technique over the long term.

- I will not be ashamed to say "I know not" nor will I fail to recommend others when the skills of another are needed for a customer's success.

- I will remember that I am not here to create a sales chart, or a short-term sale, but instead to be genuinely helpful to a human being, whose needs may affect many other factors in their life.

- I will remember that I remain a member of society, with special obligations to all my fellow human beings: I am not here to 'sell', I am here to 'add value' in the strong and constant belief that, if I do this excellently, the sales will follow: not the other way round.

- I will seek and welcome genuine feedback and seek to find value in it to help me and my team continually improve, innovate and excel.

- May I always act so as to preserve the professionalism of my calling and may I long experience the joy of helping those who seek my help.

For the sake of brevity and clarity, we can precis this to:

- I am a member of society, with special obligations to all my fellow human beings: I am not here to 'sell', I am here to 'add value' in the strong and constant belief that, if I do this excellently, the sales will follow: not the other way round.

- May I always act so as to preserve the professionalism of my calling and may I long experience the joy of earning trust and loyalty from those who seek my help.

- The 4 key guiding principles to achieve this are:

    1. To be **'Genuinely Helpful'** in all I do

    2. To build **'Quality & Value'** in all transactions

    3. To offer **'Honest Solutions'** at all times

4. To **'Welcome Feedback'** to help me continually improve.

Note: these 4 principles, align with the 4 'BEAR' principles of human behaviour, as set out in the book 'Slow Selling':

Beliefs: *to be **'Genuinely Helpful'** (in the belief that: 'If I do this well, then the sales will follow ... not the other way round').*

Emotions: *to build **'Quality & Value'** (remembering that these are emotional judgements made by my customer: they are not determined by me).*

Actions: *to offer **'Honest Solutions'** (by using a win/win process in small steps with the customer).*

Results: *to **'Welcome Feedback'** (to measure my success using the 'lead measure' of feedback to hold myself accountable, build customer loyalty and drive continuous improvement in my offer).*

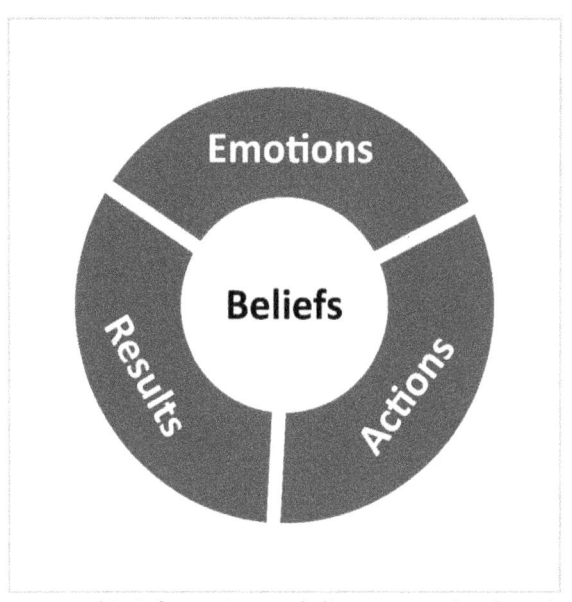

Please note: this information and diagram can be downloaded from the Slow Sellers association at www.slow-sellers.org